MW00668253

MORE THAN PETTICOATS

Remarkable Pennsylvania Women

Kate Hertzog

TWODOT®

GUILFORD, CONNECTICUT
HELENA, MONTANA
AN IMPRINT OF THE GLOBE PEQUOT PRESS

A · T W O D O T® · B O O K

Text design by Nancy Freeborn
Map created by M. A. Dubé © Morris Book Publishing, LLC
Front cover photo: A crew of female engine cleaners on the Pennsylvania Railroad during World War II. Library of Congress, LC-USW33-025835-C.
Back cover photo: Socially prominent women and their daughters playing baseball at the Shady Hill Country Day School, Chestnut Hill, Pennsylvania (Mrs. Sydney E. Martin batting and Polly Lewis catching, with the mother's bench in the background). Library of Congress, LC-DIG-ppmsca-06615.

Library of Congress Cataloging-in-Publication Data is available.
ISBN 978-0-7627-3637-9

Manufactured in the United States of America
First Edition/First Printing

In memory of my mother,
Joan T. Jones

I was blessed to have you
as my mother.
And even more blessed to have you as my friend.

I miss you, Mom.

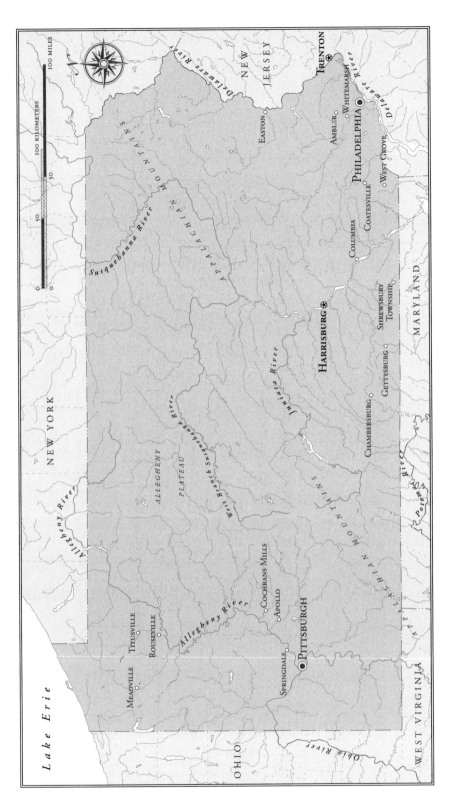

PENNSYLVANIA

CONTENTS

ACKNOWLEDGMENTS

I urge anyone who hasn't been to the library lately to reconnect with this American institution. While conducting research for this book, I discovered my library card was a gateway to a wealth of information, including online encyclopedias, articles, and research databases. The Access Pennsylvania system allowed me to find research material in public, school, and special libraries throughout the state and then request to have the information sent to my local library. I owe a special thanks to all the research librarians who worked on my interlibrary loans—your efforts made my gathering information from throughout the state a manageable endeavor.

I would also like to thank my good friend and former college roommate, Becky Snyder DiRosa, for all the feedback she gave on my work in progress. And there aren't enough words to thank my husband, Tim, who not only gave me valuable insight and feedback on my work but also kept our life running smoothly while I was lost in the writing process. Thanks for all your support, and for giving so freely of yourself without complaining—I only hope I can be as gracious if the tables are ever turned.

This book would not be in your hands today without the efforts of the dedicated staff at Globe Pequot Press; thanks to everyone who had a part in its formation. Special thanks go to managing editor Amy Paradysz and copy editor Paulette Baker for their insightful feedback during the editing process.

INTRODUCTION

I can't imagine living in a world where I would be considered inferior in any way because I'm a woman. Although sexism still exists, American culture promotes the equality of women and men as a fact. There are laws against discrimination on the basis of sex and against sexual harassment, and women are now encouraged to speak up for themselves.

But there was a time in America when women were widely viewed as second-class citizens, and it wasn't that long ago. The nineteenth amendment, which gave women the right to vote, was adopted on August 26, 1920—less than one hundred years ago. All the women you'll read about in this book were born at least a decade before that historic date, and some were born more than a century before it. Many had to overcome obstacles that were in their paths only because of their gender, and all had to live in a world where it was widely felt women were not as capable as men in many aspects of life.

Often this bias led to women's accomplishments being mitigated when men wrote the history of their day, and no doubt many remarkable deeds by women were never recorded. Luckily, diaries and correspondence written by women have been able to fill in many of the gaps in the history books, and today more and more women's stories are coming to light.

This book shines a sliver of light on fifteen of the many women of Pennsylvania who deserve to be called remarkable. Pennsylvania's rich history, dating from 1681, provided a plethora of women whose stories made including only fifteen difficult. The women whose lives

I explore here were selected because something about them spoke to me. I wanted to be sure they were recognized for what they did, and I often struggled to capture the magnitude of their acts on paper.

The stories presented also serve as small snapshots of American history. Sometimes the women made history with their deeds, and other times their actions were reflections of the times they lived in. They come from across the state of Pennsylvania, and their occupations range from housewife to soldier to businesswoman to scientist.

Each woman featured displayed courage and a belief in her abilities. I hope their stories have as profound an effect on you as they did on me.

SYBILLA MASTERS

1676–1720

American Inventor

As she watched the Native-American women grind up corn, Sybilla Masters wondered if their method was better than the way the colonists currently prepared their corn for cooking. Sybilla was always wondering things like that, always looking for a better way to do things. With four children, a husband, and two houses to run, Sybilla had her hands full. Life in colonial Pennsylvania in the early 1700s was not easy—many of the people who are today famous for inventing items we now take for granted, such as electricity, inside plumbing, and ovens, had not even been born yet. Although Sybilla and her husband were well off financially and probably had servants, Sybilla still had to oversee a household abuzz with activity. Fires, which were used for heating and cooking, had to be built and tended to, clothes needed to be made and mended, and food needed to be prepared and cooked. Any food served in colonial times was truly made from scratch.

The Native Americans had introduced the first settlers in the colonies to corn, and its abundance in the New World made it a staple on dining tables in colonial times. But corn could not be eaten raw. The corn first had to be dried and then soaked in lye water usually made from wood ash so that the outer hull could be easily removed. Once the hull was gone, the corn was shelled and pulverized and the resulting fine flour was separated from the coarse meal. Hominy was made with the coarse meal, a food item that was probably served in every colonial household during the early 1700s.

The colonists used two large stones, called millstones, to grind the corn, but the Native Americans Sybilla was watching were pounding the corn with large wooden posts. Sybilla decided to try their method, and she did find it to be easier. But rather than just adopting the method the Native Americans used, Sybilla began to experiment with ways to perfect the process. After much trial and error, she had a new method figured out. She built a long cylinder out of wood and placed projections on each side. The projections made a series of heavy pestles drop onto mortars that were filled with kernels of corn. The heavy pestles ground the corn into finer grain than when the corn was ground by stones, and the entire contraption could be powered by either horses or a waterwheel.

By trying to turn an arduous job into an easier one, Sybilla invented a mill and became the first known American women inventor. But Sybilla wasn't done inventing yet. She also created a process where she weaved straw and palmetto leaves from the West Indies into hats. She was quite unconventional for her time, when women usually left the building of cylinders and mortars and such to men.

Sybilla didn't believe herself to be in any way less than any man, and she had confidence in her abilities as an inventor. No doubt much of her inner fortitude came from her being raised as a Quaker, a religion founded in the mid-seventeenth century whose central message was that each person had an inner light that allowed them to have a personal relationship with God. Quakers were taught to always listen to this inner voice and to demonstrate their faith by doing good deeds as they lived their daily lives. They believed in the equality of all people, and they applied their religion to all aspects of their lives.

Sybilla was born sometime in 1676 in the English colony of Bermuda. Her parents were William and Sarah Righton, and Sybilla was the second of their seven children. When Sybilla was around eleven years old, her family moved to the American colonies and settled in West New Jersey. Her father bought a plantation along the Delaware River that he named "Bermuda." This is where Sybilla spent her early life, and it is also where she first witnessed prejudice against Quakers.

West New Jersey was populated mostly by people who belonged to the Anglican church, and some did not like having Quakers in their midst. Many of the Quakers were landowners, and some of the officials of New Jersey tried to find ways to take away their land. Sybilla's name appears in court documents from 1692 when she testified on behalf of her father in court. In 1693 the Society of Friends, as the Quakers were officially called, in the area banded together and organized the West Jersey Council of Proprietors in order to protect their landowning rights. Some officials of the area, who were Anglican, were trying to deny the Quakers the right to vote, which would give the Anglicans control over land purchases and sales. The government of England had to step in to ensure that the Quakers were allowed to retain their voting rights.

Around this time Sybilla met and married Thomas Masters, who was also a Quaker. Thomas Masters was originally from Bermuda, so he and Sybilla had a common origin of birth as well as sharing the same religion. He had emigrated from Bermuda to Philadelphia, in the colony of Pennsylvania, in 1685. There Thomas was a well-to-do merchant and landowner, and he took Sybilla to Philadelphia to live after their marriage. In Philadelphia Sybilla would not feel any prejudice because of her being a Quaker; she would be surrounded by other Quakers. After all, Pennsylvania had been founded by William Penn, also a Quaker, in 1681 with the intent that all colonists who lived there would do so with political and religious freedom. Penn himself helped to lay out the town of Philadelphia in 1682, and he made it the capital of the colony. At the time Sybilla arrived in the hometown of her new husband, Philadelphia was still in its infancy, but the city was important from its first inception. The name Philadelphia means brotherly love, and William Penn designed it to be a model of his Quaker belief of tolerance toward the religious beliefs of others. For this reason, many Quakers chose Pennsylvania, and especially Philadelphia, as their home.

Sybilla and Thomas prospered in Philadelphia. By 1702 they had built a home along Philadelphia's riverfront, and it was so impressive that William Penn's secretary, James Logan, described it as "the most substantial fabric in the town." They also had a home on a plantation the family owned outside of town. At this time of early immigration to Philadelphia, anyone who bought land in the city also received farmland in the surrounding countryside. William Penn had planned this to allow city dwellers to relax in the country. Thomas Masters became active in city politics, first serving as an alderman and then as mayor from 1707 to 1708. This prosperity no doubt allowed Sybilla to make the decision she did on June 24, 1712, when she told her Quaker meeting that she wanted to travel to London and receive patents for her new way of working with corn and her way of weaving straw. Her meeting supported her by giving her a certificate of good standing to take with her as a form of introduction, and Sybilla shortly set out for England. She knew she would have to get the patent in the name of her husband because women were not allowed to obtain a patent in their own names at the time. Technically wives were considered the property of their husbands, but Thomas was a good husband and a good Quaker and believed in equality between the sexes. He always made clear to those he met that his wife was responsible for inventing a new way of pulverizing corn and the process of weaving straw and palmetto leaves into hats.

Deciding to patent an invention was a new and bold idea in 1712. Some of the colonies in the New World were issuing patents, but Pennsylvania was not among them. And even many colonists who lived in colonies that issued patents felt it was best to receive a patent from England because England ruled the American colonies. Men receiving patents was not common, and the fact that Sybilla was a woman seeking a patent was a true anomaly. Sybilla must have been very strong in her convictions to leave four children and a husband behind and sail to England on her own. The sea journey was very long, and she found out when she reached London that there was no formal procedure for acquiring these new ownership rights called patents. She worked through all the tangled rules and regulations, or lack thereof, and eventually she applied directly to King George I for her patents. Then her wait began.

A reply to her request would take three long years, time that Sybilla would remain in London. By staying abroad alone, Sybilla was ignoring all the social norms of the day. Although she was well-to-do and moved in the same social circles as Hannah Penn, William Penn's wife, Sybilla's actions were still found to be appalling by most who knew her. In a letter to James Logan dated April 2, 1716, Hannah wrote: "I hope Sybilla Masters will also return to hers, all her friends, I believe, in these parts wish it and I hope she is prevailed on to attempt it for the good of herself and family."

Sybilla would come home from London in 1716, but it would not be because society frowned on women leaving a husband and four children for any reason, let alone for one of a business nature. It would be because she had been successful in her endeavor. King George I granted patent number 401 on November 25, 1715. The patent was granted to Thomas Masters, but its wording left no doubt that Sybilla was the actual inventor. The patent states that it's granted for " . . . the sole use and benefit of a new invention found out by Sybilla, his wife, for cleaning and curing the Indian corn growing in the several colonies in America." The second patent, number 403, was granted, again in Thomas's name, on February 18, 1716. The patent's official title was "Working and Weaving in a New Method, Palmetta Chip and Straw for Hats and Bonnets and other improvements of that Ware."

Once the patents were received, both Thomas and Sybilla put them to immediate use. Sybilla got a permit that gave her a monopoly on importing the leaves from the West Indies that she used in her weaving of hats. She then opened a business in London, another action quite out of the ordinary for a woman in those times. Within her shop she sold hats and bonnets made using the new weaving process, and she eventually applied the method to making chair covers, baskets, and matting for floors and furniture, which she also sold in her store. The store was called the West Indies Hat and Bonnet, and prices began at one shilling, according to an advertisement of March 18, 1716, that appeared in the *London Gazette.*

Back in the American colonies, Thomas had bought what was called "the Governor's mill" in 1714 along the Cohocksink Creek and was implementing Sybilla's new design for pulverizing corn. (The mill got its name from having been built originally for William Penn.) The end product of the milling process was called "Tuscarora Rice." The mill's design operated well, and Thomas and Sybilla planned to distribute the Tuscarora rice to a wide market. Although it was basically a food product, they also marketed Tuscarora rice to Philadelphians as a cure for tuberculosis. The plan was to sell the rice as both a medicine and a food, but it turned out that people did not particularly like the taste of this new product, and sales were light. Eventually sales dwindled to the point that Thomas sold the mill.

Sybilla returned to Philadelphia on May 25, 1716. She had been gone almost four years, and she spent much of her time getting reacquainted with her husband and children. The patents were recorded and published in Philadelphia, an extra precaution taken to ensure ownership of the inventions in the colonies. Once again, the patents were granted in Thomas's name, but it was common knowledge that Sybilla was the true inventor.

Besides being the first known American woman inventor, Sybilla was also the first person from the American colonies to obtain a patent from the king of England. She was an extraordinary woman who showed great ingenuity and self-confidence at a time when most women fulfilled traditional roles of wife and mother by quietly running households. Her husband was also quite extraordinary. Not only did he consider his wife his equal, but he also was willing to give her full credit for her inventions.

The American colonies would not operate their own patent office until 1793, and a woman would not be granted a patent in her own name until 1809. Mary Dixon Kies, who was from Connecticut, would have that honor with a patent reminiscent of Sybilla's second patent. It would be for a new way of weaving straw using silk, and the process would be used to make hats.

By 1860, 140 years after Sybilla's death, only fifty-two women had applied for and been granted patents by the U.S. Patents office. All of these women had to be self-assured and courageous, but none as much as Sybilla, who blazed the trail for those who followed.

LYDIA DARRAGH

1728-1789

House Spy

HER HEART WAS THUMPING AGAINST HER CHEST so hard Lydia thought it might actually rip right through her skin. Or worse, one of the soldiers behind the door she stood at might hear its thumping, fling the door open, and discover her standing there in her bed-clothes. Slowly she made herself breathe evenly, made her heart beat slower, and made herself concentrate on what was being said inside the room.

As the words wafted through the door, Lydia knew she had been right to think this gathering was different from other meetings the British soldiers had held in their house since taking over Philadelphia in September 1777. That had been two months ago, and when the soldier told her earlier that day to have her family retire by 8:00 p.m. and remain in their bedchambers for the night, Lydia's curiosity was piqued. The British soldiers never requested that the family remain in their rooms while they met; in fact, they usually talked quite freely around the Darraghs, who were Quak-ers—a religious sect whose overwhelmingly pacifist members remained neutral when it came to matters of war.

Before the full impact of the words she had heard sunk in, Lydia once again listened intently in the hope that more details would be given. But instead she heard the creaking of chairs as men stood up, and Lydia quickly fled to her bed as the meeting adjourned. There she stared at the ceiling as her husband, William, slept beside her. She waited for the knock on her door that she expected at any moment as she heard boots clattering on the floors as the men left the house. When the knock finally came after what seemed like minutes but actually was probably only a few seconds, she forced herself to lie still until two more sharp raps had sounded. Then she got out of bed and acted as she answered the door as though she had just awakened. The British soldier who stood there obviously believed her act as he told her the meeting was over, the soldiers were leaving, and she was to lock up the house and put out the fires.

Lydia completed the household chores and returned to her bed, and all the while the words she had overheard reverberated in her head. The British were going to attack General Washington's troops on the fourth—and this was the night of the second. The attack was to happen at Whitemarsh, about twelve miles away, in the Valley Forge area. Lydia was awake a long time praying over what to do. When she awoke the next day her thoughts were still in a tumble, and she had decided only one thing: She would not involve anyone else in whatever she did. She didn't tell William what she had heard, and she decided against trying to send a message to her son Charles, who was a lieutenant stationed with Washington's army. Lydia knew William would be against her getting involved in anything this dangerous, and she would never forgive herself if Charles were captured relaying her message to General Washington. She had heard of men being chased down by British cavalrymen and hanged on just the suspicion of spying. Besides, she was the one who had heard the words, so she should be the one to carry them. That way she wouldn't have to put the words down on paper.

Although this would not be the first time Lydia sent a message to the troops about British activities, it would be the first time she herself carried a message. When General Howe took control of Philadelphia, then the largest city in the colonies, for the British on September 26, 1777, he set up his headquarters in the house across the street from the Darraghs, and Lydia diligently observed all the activities she could from a vantage point at her window. About a month later, General Howe decided to also requisition the Darraghs's house, which was located at 177 South Second Street and called the Loxley House. A soldier showed up one evening and informed Lydia that her family was to leave the house—General Howe's headquarters were expanding. After much cajoling, Lydia managed to convince General Howe that he needed only part of the house, and it was decided that the parlor would be used for staff meetings. Lydia and William, their twenty-year-old daughter Ann, and their fourteen-year-old son John were allowed to remain in the house, but the general sent Lydia's two younger children to stay with relatives of hers who lived in the countryside. Lydia and her family were firsthand observers of the activities that went on at General Howe's headquarters, and when Lydia saw something interesting she told William, who put what she had told him on paper in code. The papers were then hidden behind the buttons of son John's coat, and John carried the messages to Charles on the pretense of running some errand for Lydia.

Whitemarsh, at twelve miles away, was not a great distance for a boy of fourteen to travel, but it seemed a very great distance to Lydia, who was almost fifty years old and described by contemporaries as frail, soft-spoken, and feminine. But she was determined not to let the soldiers at Whitemarsh be routed by the British, and as she and William retired for the evening, she put her plan in motion. She told William that she wanted to leave early the next morning to get flour at the Frankford Mill and visit their younger children in the countryside. William didn't want Lydia to travel such a distance by herself, but she adamantly refused to take the maid along, and eventually he gave in to her wishes.

When Lydia awoke the next morning, she slipped out of bed quietly and silently gave thanks that William was still fast asleep. She wanted to be gone quickly. She was anxious to get word to the troops of the impending attack, and she wanted to be sure William didn't awaken, change his mind, and tell her not to go. Being as quiet as she could, Lydia dressed in her everyday clothes: a gray wool dress, wool stockings, and pointed leather shoes. She placed her white kerchief on her head, tugged the lappets over her ears, put on her hooded wool cloak, and hurried out the door clutching an empty flour sack.

As the coldness of the early December morning hit her, she realized that it was very early—maybe too early. Other than a few sentinels at the street corners, Lydia was alone. She wondered if her presence so early in the day would arouse suspicion and worried that she had already botched her plan. Well, there was no turning back now. Lydia began walking briskly, and as she shoved her hands in her pockets to protect them from the cold, her hand closed around the pass that allowed her to leave the city limits to pick up flour. She also felt the pass she had received from General Howe that allowed her to visit her children in the countryside. She had missed her children since they had been sent away by General Howe, but her loss was to turn out to be a godsend for the colonial troops. Visiting her children would supply Lydia with a perfect reason to give any soldiers she happened upon if they asked why she was in the countryside, or if she had to explain the length of time she would be away.

She met her first patrol about an hour later on the Germantown Road. She told her story of going to the Franklin Mill for flour and stopping to see her children, and the guard looked through her bag and asked to see her papers. Although it seemed to take the soldier a very long time to study the folded sheets she handed him, he finally returned them and waved her on. Lydia would go through many similar scenarios as she made her way to the mill, five miles from town. Once there, she dropped off her bag and placed her order for flour.

Knowing that she had until sundown to come back for the bag without causing any speculation, Lydia took a few moments to breathe in the country air and relish the fact that she was no longer within British-held territory. Then she gathered her stamina and began traveling Nicetown Lane westward. Her destination was the Rising Sun Tavern, three miles away at the intersection of Old York and Germantown Roads. The tavern was a known meeting place where messages often were passed to the troops, a fact that led to Lydia being quite scared a while later when she saw a man on horseback approaching from the other direction. She had no doubt she would be harshly questioned about her reasons for being on the road that led to the tavern if the figure coming toward her was a British scout. She was quite relieved when the horseman turned out to be an American officer she knew, a Colonel Craig. He, in turn, was quite surprised to see her almost six miles from town.

When Colonel Craig asked what she was doing so far from town, Lydia asked him to walk beside her, and the urgency in her voice compelled the officer to dismount immediately. He led his horse as he walked beside Lydia, and she quickly told him about the meeting that had been held at her house and what she had heard of the British plan to attack the troops at Whitemarsh that evening. The colonel led Lydia to a nearby farmhouse, where he ordered the owner to see that she was fed and allowed to rest. He assured Lydia that he would get her message to General Washington, and he quickly rode away on his horse toward the Rising Sun Tavern.

Unbeknownst to Lydia, Colonel Craig was active in the intelligence gathering being done by some Americans in the area around

Lydia Darrah Giving Warning.

From an engraving in *Godey's Lady's Book*, 1845.

LYDIA DARRAGH WARNS THE CONTINENTAL ARMY

Philadelphia. When he arrived at the tavern, Col. Elias Boudinot, the head of Washington's spy ring, was having dinner. Colonel Craig passed the information he had been given to Colonel Boudinot, who ensured that it was received by General Washington.

After replenishing her energy with food and rest, Lydia left the farmhouse and began walking back to the mill to gather the flour she had ordered. It was a long and cold walk, and Lydia kept praying that the colonel would reach General Washington in time. Once she left the mill, her twenty-five-pound sack of flour made the remaining five-mile walk almost unbearable, but thoughts of her Charles and the other boys at Whitemarsh—and to no small effect the thought of being found out to be a spy—spurred her on. She was greatly relieved when she arrived home without arousing anyone's suspicions. In total, she had walked more than twelve miles that day.

About 11:00 p.m. Lydia sat at her front window wrapped in a cloak, unable to sleep knowing that the British soldiers would be leaving to attack Whitemarsh at any time. She soon heard the unmistakable sound of soldiers' boots and artillery pieces as they moved through town. But as she listened, she realized the sounds were traveling in a direction opposite Whitemarsh. Now Lydia didn't know what to think. She briefly wondered if she had heard the words correctly two nights ago as she listened through the door. No, she was sure she had relayed exactly what she had heard. Had the plans changed? Or had the British soldiers realized Lydia had been listening and perhaps said things so she would feed the colonial army the wrong information? Did they know Lydia was a spy? All these thoughts filled Lydia's mind, but she knew she had no choice but to wait and see what transpired over the course of the next few days.

It would take many days for news of the fighting to reach Philadelphia. The British army had indeed marched in the opposite direction of Whitemarsh as they left Philadelphia on the night of

December fourth. This was intended as a ruse, and the troops circled back toward Whitemarsh once they were a distance from Philadelphia. But to their surprise, the British found the American troops poised for battle when they reached Whitemarsh. Both sides dug in, and the British eventually concluded that their only hope for victory would entail making a frontal assault on the Revolutionary troops, a daring move that General Howe was not prepared to initiate after the losses he had incurred when he had attempted a similar maneuver at the Battle of Bunker Hill. Instead, General Howe ordered the retreat of the British troops to Philadelphia on the eighth of December.

As the beleaguered soldiers returned to town, Lydia knew from the rumblings she heard that the military felt the Americans had known they were coming. General Howe and his men began scouting throughout town looking for leads on who was responsible for the leak of information. Lydia continued about her household chores, but shortly thereafter she received a summons to speak with a British officer. She made her way to his council chamber, which had been until recently just the parlor in her own house. When she arrived, the officer offered her a chair; she took a seat and felt momentarily dazed by how quickly life could change: Before the army had commandeered her house, the chair she sat on had always been hers to offer.

She sat quietly with her hands folded, the picture of a demure Quaker woman, dressed in her standard gray dress and white cap. Inwardly, her thoughts were racing and she was afraid she might faint. She clenched her hands tighter in her lap and gave thanks that the room was dark; she was afraid the soldier might realize her guilt if he looked too closely at her face. Lydia was not sure if she could tell a lie; she had never attempted to do so before.

"Was anyone in your family awake the night of our last council?" the officer asked, and Lydia honestly answered, "No, they were all in bed asleep." The soldier commented that he didn't need to ask Lydia if she had been asleep because he knew she had needed to be awakened to lock the house door as the soldiers left the council. Lydia remained quiet and kept her eyes down, and the officer took her silence as agreement. After a few more moments, the meeting was concluded.

The British never found out who had foiled their plan. After spending the winter in relative comfort in Philadelphia while the Continental Army camped at Valley Forge, the British troops pulled out of Philadelphia in June 1778 as part of an overall plan to consolidate their forces in the New York area. With their departure, the need for spying was over and Lydia went back to her normal routine of taking care of her husband and children and attending meetings of the Friends, as the Quakers called themselves.

Until the time of her espionage, Lydia had led a quiet life. She was born around 1728 and raised in Dublin, Ireland, as part of a large and loving family. William Darragh, the son of a clergyman, was the family tutor, and he and Lydia fell in love and married on November 2, 1753, in a Quaker celebration. Lydia was twenty-five, and William was thirty-four years old. The couple soon moved to the colonies and made Philadelphia their home, as did many Quakers of the time. They became well-known members of the Monthly Meeting of Friends in Philadelphia, and both were considered devout Quakers.

William worked as a tutor, and Lydia eventually gave birth to nine children, four of whom died in infancy. The five surviving children were Charles, born in 1755; Ann, born in 1757; John, born in 1763; William, born in 1766; and Susannah, born in 1768.

Lydia was busy running her household and taking care of her children when the Revolutionary War began. Many of her fellow Quakers were quite surprised when her oldest son, Charles, decided to enlist in the army. But Lydia and her family did not have a moral dilemma with it. Although Quakers were expected to be neutral in the war, they also believed that all human beings were entitled to freedom. Lydia, and her husband and family, felt the colonists were right in their quest to govern their own land. Of course Lydia kept her opinions on the conflict to herself, and even after the war she told only a few close friends and family of her adventure. Her daughter Ann, who was twenty-one at the time Lydia made her twelve-mile trek "for flour," transcribed her mother's story onto paper in 1827.

After William died on June 8, 1783, Lydia fell out of favor with the Society of Friends. Two months after William was buried in the Friends Burial Ground at Fourth and Arch Streets in Philadelphia, Lydia lost her membership in the Friends Meeting House because she was neglecting to attend the meetings. In 1786 Lydia purchased property on the west side of Second Street, where she lived and ran a store until her death on December 28, 1789, at the age of sixty-one. Although her ties with the Society of Friends had been severely tested by her past actions, she was buried in the Friends Burial Ground at Fourth and Arch Streets.

Although for fifty years Lydia's story was taught in schools and considered to have come from trustworthy sources, in 1877 some newspapers cast doubt on the credibility of Lydia's story by questioning the likelihood of the events in her narrative. One fact is not in dispute: Washington's army at Whitemarsh was ready and waiting when British troops under the command of General Howe attacked on the night of December 4, 1777. Although this could be a coincidence, it seems more likely that Lydia, a frail woman of forty-nine years of age, did indeed get word of a surprise attack to General Washington.

Lydia certainly is not the picture that comes to mind when one imagines a spy taking a message through enemy lines. Her story proves the adage that one shouldn't judge a book by its cover or, in Lydia's case, by its religion.

MARGARET CORBIN

1754-1800

Half-Soldier, Full Hero

ON THE MORNING OF NOVEMBER 16, 1776, Margaret Corbin surveyed the line of colonial troops that wound before her as she waited in the anticipatory lull she had learned always preceded a battle. The line supposedly went on for almost five miles and encircled Fort Washington, which was on the northern tip of Manhattan Island in an area known as Harlem Heights in New York. Margaret's husband was a private with the First Company of Pennsylvania Artillery, which was stationed at the fort. When the majority of the Continental Army had withdrawn weeks earlier from Manhattan Island to White Plains, New York, the Continental Congress had decided that a garrison should remain behind to man Fort Washington. Set on a bluff 230 feet above the Hudson River, the fort was the last stronghold held by colonial troops on Manhattan Island, and artillery forces used the fort's high vantage point to rain cannonballs down on British ships traveling on the river below.

Margaret looked up at Fort Washington from her spot on the small outer redoubt named Forest Hill, and then she peered down and tried to spy the British and Hessian troops she knew were gathering below her. She watched diligently for the distinctive red coats of the British uniform or for the caps, tricorne hats, or leather-crested helmets the soldiers wore. She also kept an eye out for the German infantry, or Hessians, who fought on the side of the British. They usually wore blue coats and miter with brass front plates on their heads. She was able to make out the British frigate *Pearl* in the Hudson waters below. As Margaret's gaze swept across the colonial forces, she noted that most wore civilian clothes, although a few were beginning to wear blue coats and pants to identify themselves as part of the army. The majority of troops at the fort were from Pennsylvania, with the colonies of Virginia and Maryland also represented.

Margaret knew the men defending the fort were greatly outnumbered. Rather than following General Washington and the main body of the Continental Army when it withdrew after its loss at White Plains, the British troops had regrouped at Manhattan Island. They were feeling confident after their recent victories and had decided to put an end to the constant shelling they endured from the fort. The latest estimates on troop strengths set the British forces at around 8,000 soldiers, an overwhelming advantage over the 2,900 colonial soldiers in place. Yesterday British commander General Howe had offered to allow the colonial forces to surrender, but the offer was immediately rejected by Fort Washington's commanding officer, Colonel Magaw.

From that point, everyone knew the fight would begin this morning. Margaret followed her husband to his assigned two-gun battery as he and the rest of the colonial troops manned their weapons and prepared for battle in the dawn of the new day. Two regiments of colonial troops prepared to hold off enemy troops who would advance from the Hudson River to the west, over land from the north, and from the Harlem River to the east. There were roughly three enemy men for every man fighting for the Continental Army.

This was not the first battle Margaret had experienced. In 1776 her husband, John Corbin, had enlisted with Capt. Thomas Proctor's First Company of Pennsylvania Artillery, Continental Line, which had been formed on October 16, 1775, for the defense of Pennsylvania. When John told Margaret of his enlistment, she announced that he was not going off to war without her. Margaret was almost twenty-five years old; she and John had been married for four years but had no children. She felt she had a better chance of surviving financially with the army than on her own, so she rolled her belongings up in a blanket and joined the many other women and children who traveled with the troops. The First Company of Pennsylvania Artillery was under Pennsylvania's control until it was absorbed into General Washington's Continental Army on June 6, 1777. The company had already seen many conflicts over the past year, and Margaret, a robust woman who stood five feet, eight inches tall, felt her strength and endurance expand as she traveled with her husband.

It was not unusual for women and children to travel with the troops during the Revolutionary War, and the people who followed the soldiers were called camp followers. Margaret had heard that General Washington didn't approve of the practice, and she knew that many in society looked down on her, but Margaret felt that the camp followers served a vital function. While traveling with the troops, Margaret and the other women cooked, washed dishes, did laundry, mended clothes, and tended to the soldiers' minor medical needs. In return for their work, the camp followers were provided with food and shelter, and in some regiments they were paid a small amount. They traveled as a group behind the regular army when it was on the march. Camp followers endured the same hardships as the enlisted men. Food was sometimes not plentiful or not very appetizing, and the marches they endured were exhausting.

Besides completing the traditional tasks done by women, Margaret also spent time watching her husband and the rest of the men

MARGARET CORBIN IN A SKETCH BY
HERBERT KNÖTEL

who made up a gun crew when they conducted artillery drills. The men noted her interest and eventually taught her how to swab out the cannon between shots and reload it. Although most of the camp followers stayed in camp when the soldiers went to battle, some women entered into the fray at their husbands' sides. These camp followers were sometimes called half-soldiers. Margaret was a half-soldier, and she had been beside her husband each time he had manned his cannon in battle. So far their life with the army had taken them from their home outside Chambersburg, Pennsylvania, to their present location on Forest Hill, where they were preparing to defend Fort Washington against overwhelming odds.

The battle began a little after 7:00 a.m. on November 16. Margaret heard the sounds of warfare in the distance, and John and the gunner began preparing their cannon. Hessian infantry led by Lt. Gen. Wilhelm Baron von Knyphausen were climbing up their hill at an alarming rate. Although the colonial troops fought valiantly, their numbers could not match the enemy's as the three-pronged attack by the British and Hessian soldiers proved devastatingly effective. Soon the slope of Forest Hill was being overrun by Hessians, and Margaret heard shells whizzing by as the battery was besieged by enemy fire. She kept her eyes on her husband and the gunner as they fired their cannon again and again. After each shot, John, who served as the matross, would clean the cannon chamber, load the next round and pack it down tightly, and then signal the gunner to light the gunpowder.

Suddenly Margaret saw the gunner fall to the ground. When Margaret realized he was too hurt to continue firing the cannon, she immediately sprang into action and ran to John's side. She took the matross's position at the cannon as John took over for the wounded gunner. Margaret quickly loaded the gunpowder and grapeshot, packed it tightly with the ramrod, and gave John the signal to light the gunpowder. The cannon exploded into action; Margaret once again began the loading process as the British army continued to advance on their position. Then she saw her husband struck down by a mortal blow. Without hesitating, Margaret stepped over his body and took over his cannon duties as well. She was now loading and firing the cannon, a job usually done by two men, and she was doing it with a battle raging all around her. Margaret continued manning her gun until enemy fire made a direct hit on her position, and she fell to the ground with her left arm almost severed and her left breast and the left side of her face mangled by grapeshot.

Margaret lay wounded on the field of battle as the British troops overwhelmed the colonial forces. The Americans' weapons were being fired so fast they began to overheat, and they withdrew to Fort Washington. Colonel Magaw eventually realized the situation was hopeless and surrendered Fort Washington to the British. After four hours, the Battle of Fort Washington had come to an end. The defeat meant the imprisonment of more than 2,800 colonial troops, with nearly 100 of them being wounded. On the afternoon of the battle, a doctor walking the battlefield looking for casualties was quite surprised to find the badly wounded Margaret Corbin. Margaret was taken prisoner but soon turned over to the Continental Army. She was loaded onto a wagon with other seriously injured soldiers and sent to Philadelphia, a bone-jarring journey of almost one hundred miles.

Margaret, now a widow, survived her injuries but never recovered the use of her left arm, which meant she could not support herself financially. She eventually enrolled in the Invalid Regiment, a regiment of disabled soldiers that was formed by the Continental Congress on June 20, 1777, and assigned to West Point. Margaret was allowed to join the regiment, which did not fight but instead did light jobs, even though she had never enlisted as a soldier in the army. During her time with the Invalid Regiment, Margaret got the nickname Captain Molly. She always wore an artilleryman's coat over her dress, and she was described as being irritable and quarrel-some by more than one acquaintance. Captain Molly insisted that enlisted men salute her, and she would return their salute with a snappy one of her own. She also received a daily ration of rum, just as the men of the Invalid Regiment did, and it's been noted that she sometimes smoked a clay pipe.

On June 29, 1779, the Supreme Court of Pennsylvania recognized Margaret's heroism and awarded her $30 "to relieve her present necessities, she having been wounded and utterly disabled by three grapeshot, when she filled with distinguished bravery the post of her husband, who was killed by her side, serving a piece of artillery at Fort Washington."

By this decree, Margaret Corbin officially became the first servicewoman of the new nation of the United States.

The court also recommended that Margaret be given further consideration by the Board of War because she was unable to earn a living due to the injury to her left arm. On July 6, 1779, Congress directed "that Margaret Corbin receive one-half the monthly pay of a soldier in the services of these States and that she now receive out of public stores one suit of clothes or the value thereof in money." By this order of Congress, Margaret became the first woman to receive a pension from the government: half the $6.33 per month pay a soldier of the time received.

Margaret remained with the Invalid Regiment until it was disbanded in 1783. Some reports have Margaret moving back to her home state of Pennsylvania at this time, but most accounts agree that she continued to make her home outside West Point in New York State. She survived on very little money, and she applied for a rum ration, which was given to soldiers but never allotted to camp followers. Margaret was awarded the rum ration, and she was also paid for rations that she had not received in the past. It appears from correspondence between Gen. Henry Knox and Quartermaster

William Price between 1782 and 1790 that Margaret continued to require special care because she couldn't bathe or dress herself due to the loss of the use of her left arm. Price arranged for Margaret to be cared for by a Mrs. Randall, who lived in the community of Highland Falls, a few miles from West Point. But Margaret's physical limitations were not her only problems—she was known to be very cantankerous. Price wrote a letter in 1795 in which he stated, "I am at a loss what to do with Capt. Molly. She is such an offensive person that people are unwilling to take her in charge." The society woman of Highland Falls had nothing to do with Margaret, who was much more comfortable in the company of the men at the post at West Point.

No doubt her injuries and widowhood had made Margaret's life a challenge, but she had endured challenges in her life from the time she was a young girl. Margaret had been born on November 12, 1751, to a Scots-Irish family outside Chambersburg, Pennsylvania, who lived in a small log cabin on a farm in an area known as Rocky Springs. When Margaret was only five years old, there was an Indian raid on Rocky Springs. Her father was killed and her mother was carried off, never to return to her family. Margaret's mother was spotted only once, about two years after her abduction and one hundred miles away from Rocky Springs.

Orphaned, Margaret and her younger brother, John, went to live with her mother's brother in the town of Shippensburg, which wasn't far from Chambersburg. She married John Corbin in 1772 at the age of twenty-one. Although John was a Virginian, the newlyweds moved closer to Margaret's childhood home and set up housekeeping near the Rocky Springs Presbyterian Church. When John died on the battlefield in 1777, the couple had been married only five years. Margaret did remarry in 1782, but her second husband was also a disabled veteran and did not live very long. Margaret passed away on January 16, 1800, and was buried by a lone cedar tree in an unmarked grave within Highland Falls Cemetery in Highland Falls, New York.

But an unmarked grave would not remain Margaret's final resting place. Tales of her heroism were passed down through generations, and in 1926 the Daughters of the American Revolution negotiated with the U.S. government to have her remains moved to West Point. On March 16, 1926, a grave detail was sent from West Point to retrieve Margaret's remains from the Highland Falls Cemetery, about five miles away. They were met by a riverboat captain who claimed that his grandfather had helped with Margaret's burial. With the captain's direction, the grave detail found the burial spot and began to dig. After much hard work digging through old tree stump roots, they finally located the remains of a box and a female skeleton that had an arm missing.

Since it was believed that Margaret had lost her left arm in her later years, all present felt this to be Margaret's remains, and the skeleton was placed in a new coffin and marched in procession to West Point. At West Point, Margaret's remains were reburied with full military honors in Section II, making her the only woman from the Revolutionary War buried at West Point, and the only woman buried there because of service in action. A monument at Margaret's grave has a bronze tablet that shows a muscular woman with flowing hair and skirts standing with a cannon rammer in her hand. The inscription reads: "In memory of Margaret Corbin, a heroine of the Revolution, known as Captain Molly, 1751–1800, who at the Battle of Fort Washington, New York, when her husband, John Corbin, was killed, kept his field piece in action until severely wounded and thereafter by act of Congress received half the pay and allowances of 'a soldier in the service.'"

As befitting the first servicewoman, there are many tributes to Margaret Corbin. Many are in the state of New York: A plaque commemorates her at Fort Tryon Park, the present-day site of Forest Hill;

the drive within the park and the circle at the southern entrance of the part where Fort Washington Avenue ends bears her name; and another plaque honoring her is within Holyrood Church on Fort Washington Avenue and 179th Street. This plaque was cast by the Daughters of the American Revolution and dedicated in 1902.

In her home state of Pennsylvania, Margaret is commemorated by a historical marker that was placed along U.S. Highway 11, 1.5 miles north of the borough of Chambersburg, in 1961. The inscription on the marker reads: "Margaret Cochran Corbin—Heroine of the Revolution; born November 12, 1751, near Rocky Spring, one and one-half miles to northwest. Accompanied her husband to war. Manned a cannon, Fort Washington, N.Y., November 16, 1776, when he was killed. She was wounded, pensioned, and assigned to invalid regiment. Died January 16, 1800; buried at West Point, N.Y."

The Shippensburg Coin Club also has honored Margaret's memory. They cast a limited-issue medal in silver and bronze in 1976 that portrayed Margaret Corbin loading a canon. One side of the coin noted that she had been born in Franklin County, Pennsylvania, that she had been wounded during the Battle of Fort Washington in New York, and that she was the only woman buried at West Point, New York, with a military combat record.

Although she was the first woman officially honored by her country for her military service, Margaret Corbin was not the only woman to step up on the field of battle and man a gun for the cause of freedom. Another Continental Army camp follower, Mary Ludwig Hays, manned her husband's cannon after he collapsed from the heat during the Battle of Monmouth, which took place in New Jersey on June 28, 1778. The two women are often confused, and indeed they do have much in common. Mary was born three years after Margaret in Carlisle, Pennsylvania, not far from Margaret's hometown of Chambersburg, Pennsylvania. Both were married to men named John who enlisted with the Pennsylvania Artillery, both were camp followers who were also half-soldiers, and both had nicknames containing the name Molly. Mary Ludwig Hays is probably better known as Molly Pitcher, a name many believe she received by carrying water in a pitcher to the thirsty men along the colonial battle lines during the Battle of Monmouth.

But the two women led drastically different lives when their participation in the Revolutionary War ended. Although Mary Hays was recognized for her service by receiving a pension and a full military burial upon her death, she basically took up her life where it had left off before her husband's enlistment. The couple returned to Pennsylvania after the war, and Mary led the conventional life of an eighteenth-century wife and mother. Margaret Corbin, though, was linked with the army for the rest of her life, and very little about her life was conventional. Margaret was a soldier to the end—a brave woman who took extraordinary actions during the Revolutionary War at great peril to herself and who would forever carry the scars of war.

Margaret showed much courage not only by taking over for her husband in the heat of battle but also by living life on her terms. After the war she made a place for herself within the military and continued to live the life of a soldier, even though that lifestyle certainly must have brought the disapproval of her female contemporaries.

LUCRETIA MOTT

1793-1880

Seeker of Equality

THERE WERE ABOUT THREE DOZEN PEOPLE standing outside when Lucretia Mott and her husband, James, reached the Wesleyan Chapel. Hiding her surprise at seeing faces of men as well as women among the group, Lucretia asked why no one had gone inside. She was not overly surprised to hear that the minister had left town with the keys. A boy was hoisted up through an open window; he unlocked the door, and the crowd streamed into the chapel. Within the next half hour, the group of three dozen swelled to almost three hundred persons.

Lucretia and the other organizers were pleasantly surprised at the robust turnout, since the announcement of the gathering to discuss women's rights had been placed in the local paper only a week before. But Lucretia Mott and Elizabeth Cady Stanton had made a vow eight years earlier to hold a convention on women's issues in the United States. The two had met at the World's Anti-Slavery Convention held in London in June 1840. Elizabeth was accompanying her husband, abolitionist Henry Stanton, who was a delegate to the convention. Lucretia was also a delegate, but at the last

moment the British decided that she and the five other women del-
egates elected by antislavery societies in the United States would
not be able to participate in the convention. The women were segregated from the men in a corner of the hall where they could not
be seen or heard. Rather than waste her time fighting for her right
to contribute, which she felt was a hopeless cause, Lucretia decided
to develop stronger ties with the other women at the convention.
She and Elizabeth had discovered they held many beliefs about
women's rights in common. Although there was an age difference
of more than twenty years between them, with Lucretia being the
elder, the two bonded immediately and began a lifelong friendship.

Lucretia and Elizabeth made their pact at a convention in London, but a tea at a friend's house proved to be the catalyst that brought
the vow to fruition. When Lucretia and James decided to visit Lucretia's sister Margaret Wright on their way home to Philadelphia after
traveling in northern New York State, the sisters had tea with Elizabeth Cady Stanton, Mary Ann McClintock, and Jane Hunt at Jane's
house on July 13, 1848. The subject of women's rights was the center of the conversation around the table, and after some discussion the
women realized that many of their complaints were similar, or that
they knew another woman with a similar complaint. The women felt
they should hold a convention to discuss the issues women had, and
by that afternoon they had placed a notice announcing the gathering
in the *Seneca County Courier* newspaper that read:

> WOMAN'S RIGHTS CONVENTION: A Convention to dis-
> cuss the social, civil, and religious conditions and rights of
> woman, will be held in the Wesleyan Chapel at Seneca Falls,
> N.Y., on Wednesday and Thursday, the 19th and 20th of July cur-
> rent, commencing at 10 o'clock a.m. During the first day the
> meeting will be exclusively for women, who are earnestly
> invited to attend. The public generally are invited to be present

on the second day when Lucretia Mott, of Philadelphia, and other ladies and gentlemen, will address the Convention.

Although the announcement said the first day was just for women, there were many men in the chapel on the nineteenth of July, and Lucretia and Elizabeth decided they should be able to stay. But their remaining at the convention created another problem. Society norms in 1848 did not allow women to preside over a gathering of men and women, so the women asked Lucretia's husband, James, to perform that function by opening the convention and introducing the speakers. He agreed, and one of the first speakers he introduced was his wife.

Lucretia, unlike the other ladies at the convention, had experience in public speaking. She was a Quaker, a religion that believed in the equality of the sexes, and she had been preaching as a Quaker minister since 1821. Lucretia explained the purpose of the convention and urged the women to participate in the debates that would soon be before them. Elizabeth Stanton then introduced the Declaration of Sentiments, which called for equal treatment of women in all aspects of society, including the home, the workplace, the church, and the political process. These declarations were the heart of the convention, and when they were voted on the next day, all but one of the declarations were unanimously accepted. The suffrage resolution was hotly debated, and when the votes were finally cast, it passed by a small margin.

Lucretia proudly stepped up to be the first to sign the Declaration of Sentiments and Resolutions, and with this document the woman's suffrage movement was officially christened. Sixty-seven women and thirty-two men added their names to Lucretia's. All of them believed that gaining equality for women would be a hard battle, as evidenced by one of the last paragraphs of the declaration, which read:

LUCRETIA MOTT

In entering upon the great work before us, we anticipate no small amount of misconception, misrepresentation, and ridicule; but we shall use every instrumentality within our power to effect our object. We shall employ agents, circulate tracts, petition the state and national legislatures, and endeavor to enlist the pulpit and the press in our behalf. We hope this Convention will be followed by a series of conventions embracing every part of the country.

The struggle for women's rights would prove to be a long and arduous one. Only one woman who signed the Declaration of Sentiments and Resolutions, Charlotte Woodward, would live long enough to vote in a political election when women were finally given the right to vote seventy-two years later.

To many women the convention at Seneca Falls was an awakening, a realization that they were equal to men and should be treated so. But Lucretia, a devout Quaker, had been taught this from the time she was a small child. The idea that men and women are equal creatures is a cornerstone of the Quaker faith, as is the belief that every individual has an inward light that guides his or her actions. Quakers belonged to Monthly Meetings, groups that met weekly to worship together. There was a minimal amount of hierarchies at the meetings, and anyone who was so moved was welcome to stand up and speak. Lucretia's firm Quaker principles led her to devote her life to social reform. Her name was mentioned in the newspaper ad for the convention at Seneca Falls because she was a well-known abolitionist, the name given to those who believed the institution of slavery should be abolished.

Born in 1793 to Quaker parents, Lucretia Coffin spent her early years in the town of Nantucket, Massachusetts, where everyday life supported the Quaker doctrines. Most of the men in town made their living from hunting sperm whales, whose oil would then be sold and made into candles and such. The men traveled great distances to hunt the whales and were often away for months or years at a time, so the women of the community were extremely self-sufficient. Lucretia would recall in a letter to Elizabeth Cady Stanton dated March 16, 1855, "During the absence of their husbands, Nantucket women have been compelled to transact business, often going to Boston to procure supplies of goods—. . . . They have kept their own accounts, & indeed acted the part of men—Then education & intellectual culture have been for years equal for girls & boys—so that their women are prepared to be companions of man in every sense—and their social circles are never divided."

Lucretia's father was a captain aboard a whaling ship, but after an especially harrowing voyage that kept him from home for more than three years, Thomas Coffin decided to give up a life at sea. In 1804 the family moved to Boston, where Thomas worked as a merchant. In 1806 it was decided that Lucretia and her younger sister Eliza would attend Nine Partners Boarding School near Poughkeepsie, New York, so the girls could get a complete education. In Boston at that time, public schools taught girls for only half the year, while boys were educated year-round.

Nine Partners was founded and run by Quakers, and Lydia's time at the school would have lifelong consequences. Elias Hicks, cofounder of the school, often gave impassioned lectures on his belief that each person should have a direct relationship with God through his own conscience, and therefore there was no need for formal traditions such as ministers, strict dogma, or sacraments within the Quaker way of life. He also gave many lectures against the institution of slavery. Both ideas ignited a fire within Lucretia, and she educated herself further on each subject.

While her head was expanding with new thoughts presented at Nine Partners, Lucretia's heart was also opening. She was attracted to James Mott Jr., a teacher at the school, who was five years her senior. After Lucretia graduated in 1808, her excellent grades caused the school to offer her a teaching position although she was only fifteen years of age, and she and James grew close during the year she taught at the school. The couple married on April 10, 1811, at the Pine Street Meetinghouse in Philadelphia, where Lucretia's family had moved in 1809. Lucretia was eighteen years old at the time of their marriage, and she and James would call Philadelphia home for the rest of their lives.

James was also a Quaker, and Lucretia and he enjoyed a happy and harmonious union. They had six children, five of whom lived to adulthood. Their second child and first son, Thomas, died of complications from a high fever in 1817, and his death had a profound effect on Lucretia and led her to begin her role as a public speaker. She spent the time after Thomas's death systematically studying the Bible, trying to understand why God had taken her son from her.

In 1818, while attending a Meeting of the Women Friends of the Western District of Philadelphia, she rose and spoke eloquently on accepting God's omnipotence when dealing with life's trials. The Quaker elders present at the meeting were impressed by Lucretia's words and demeanor, and they encouraged her to speak at future meetings. Lucretia had a natural gift for public speaking and was recognized as a minister in the Society of Friends, another name for the Quakers, in 1821. Ministers led discussions at their local meetings, and they could also travel to other meetings to preach. Lucretia was very young to achieve such an honor, but she was very well read and articulated her ideas in an organized and logical way. She spoke on Quaker issues and the burning social issues of the day, especially slavery.

Lucretia and James became firmly established in the large Quaker community in Philadelphia. At the weekly meetings Lucretia often spoke against slavery. Pennsylvania had outlawed slavery in

1800, and the United States government had outlawed the importation of slaves in 1808. Lucretia felt the next logical step should be to abolish the practice altogether, and she and her husband were active abolitionists. James was a member of the Pennsylvania Anti-Slavery Society, and Lucretia invited African Americans to her house for dinner and went with them to social functions within the city. To further support the antislavery cause, Lucretia decided not to use any products in her house that were the results of slave labor; in 1830 James followed her example and stopped the sale of cotton by his wholesale business.

Lucretia helped organize the American Anti-Slavery Society, which held its first meeting in Philadelphia during December 1833, but she wasn't allowed to sign the society's mission statement because she was a woman. Because of this, she was instrumental in founding the Philadelphia Female Anti-Slavery Society in 1833. She corresponded with other women's groups that were sprouting up throughout the country, and in 1837 she helped organize and spoke at the first Anti-Slavery Convention of American Women, which was held in New York City. Lucretia always felt that this convention was the true beginning of the women's rights movement, and she wrote to Elizabeth Cady Stanton later in life that this was where "the battle began."

Of course not everyone agreed with Lucretia's outspoken views. When the second Anti-Slavery Convention of American Women was held in Philadelphia in 1838, an angry mob burned down the meeting hall. The meeting had convened for the day and no one was hurt, but rumors spread that the mob was going to attack abolitionists in their homes. Although she was encouraged by friends to run, Lucretia remained in her house. She would later recall, "I was scarcely breathing but I felt willing to suffer whatever the cause required." Due to the quick intervention of a neighbor, the mob was unable to locate the Motts' house, and Lucretia escaped harm. While this experience may have daunted less determined people, it only served to reinforce Lucretia's dedication to the cause. She continued to speak publicly and in Quaker meetings against slavery, and she was elected as a delegate to the World's Anti-Slavery Convention in London in 1840. Here she would meet Elizabeth Cady Stanton, and the seeds of the Seneca Halls Convention in 1848 would be planted.

As more women became involved in antislavery issues, they grew more assured in their abilities to think and reason. When men would not let them be full participants in the movement, they formed their own societies. This led them to speak out for women's rights, and the social reforms of abolitionism and women's rights became closely entwined. The two causes collided in 1840 when Lucretia and Elizabeth Cady Stanton met in London at the World's Anti-Slavery Convention and bonded over the need for women's rights because Lucretia was unable to participate in the proceedings. The resulting Seneca Falls Convention, with its Declarations and Resolutions, would ignite the minds of women throughout the country.

As the women's rights movement gained momentum, Henry Dana, a prominent writer of the time, gave a series of lectures in Philadelphia where he attacked the idea that women were equal to men by quoting the Bible and prominent authors such as Shakespeare and Milton. When asked to respond, Lucretia delivered her most famous speech, "Discourse on Woman," on December 17, 1849, eloquently refuting Dana's speeches. A reporter present wrote down the entire speech, and it was eventually made into a pamphlet. "Discourse on Woman" was still being widely circulated twenty years later, and the speech can be found in its entirety on the Internet even today.

By this time Lucretia was in her mid-fifties; she had been involved in the antislavery movement for more than twenty years, and she had been speaking out for equality for all as a Quaker minister for almost thirty years. Although much of the women's movement centered on a woman's right to vote, that goal was not paramount to Lucretia. As a Quaker she wasn't interested in the political process, but she realized that as a matter of equality women should be given the right to vote, whether that right was exercised or not. Lucretia wanted women to have true equality with men, both in intellectual and social matters, and to this end she helped raise money to open the Female Medical College of Pennsylvania, the first institution of its kind in the United States. By 1860 women were making strides in many areas. They were able to more easily gain entrance to educational opportunities, and many states had passed laws that gave married women the right to control their own money. Before this, any money a woman had was considered her husband's property once they married.

The slavery question would eventually be settled by the Civil War. Although she believed every man and woman should be free, as a Quaker Lucretia was a pacifist and did not support the war. But Lucretia and James did support the antislavery cause by making their house a stop on the Underground Railroad, a decision that sometimes put their lives in danger. Lucretia realized that the ending of the war and the passing of the Thirteenth Amendment, which abolished slavery, would not automatically make African Americans equal to whites in society. She lobbied against the dissolution of the American Anti-Slavery Association, and when she lost that battle she joined the newly formed Association for the Aid and Elevation of the Freedmen, which was sponsored by the Society of Friends and had the education of African Americans and their integration into society as its goals. Once again Lucretia followed up her words with actions: When traveling she would stand on the platform that was designated for African Americans, and she insisted when land beside the Motts' property in the country was sold for development that it be racially integrated. This resulted in one of the first mixed-race communities in the nation; it was named La Mott in honor of Lucretia.

Although overshadowed by the Civil War, the women's movement continued to make strides. In May 1866 the American Equal Rights Association was formed, and Lucretia was asked to serve as its president. Despite being seventy-three years of age, Lucretia agreed, saying she "would be happy to give her name and influence if she could encourage the young and strong to carry on the good work." As she had done all her life, Lucretia corresponded with the younger women in the movement frequently, and she was considered a mentor to Elizabeth Cady Stanton and Susan B. Anthony, among others. When the members of the women's movement were torn apart by disagreement on how to deal with the language of the Fourteenth Amendment, which gave voting rights to all male citizens, she tried without success to heal the rift.

Lucretia Mott delivered her last public address in Rochester, New York, on July 19, 1878. It was the thirtieth anniversary of the Seneca Falls Convention, and Lucretia was eighty-five years old. She had lived her life by listening always to her inner light, her conscience, and this inner light had illuminated the way for her to do great things and influence much change. Her last public words summed up how she had felt her whole life about equality between the sexes: ". . . give women the privilege of cooperating in making the laws, and there will be harmony without severity, justice without oppression."

On November 11, 1880, Lucretia passed away in her sleep.

American women would achieve the right to vote forty years later, on August 26, 1920, when the Nineteenth Amendment was ratified. The first Equal Rights Amendment (ERA), which called for the elimination of discrimination on the basis of gender, was introduced in Congress in 1923. It was called the Lucretia Mott amendment in honor of all Lucretia had done to help women achieve equality with men. To date the amendment has never been ratified.

REBECCA WEBB LUKENS

1794–1854

Industrious Leader

REBECCA WEBB LUKENS SAT AT HER HUSBAND'S SIDE and tried to absorb all that had happened in the last three years. Two sons and a father lost forever. A daughter born, and another child on the way. And now her beloved husband, Charles, had taken his last breath. He had caught a fever, and suddenly he was gone. She would have to fulfill the promise she had made to him—she would have to take over the family business.

The family business was the Brandywine Iron Works, located in Coatesville, Pennsylvania, and the year was 1825. Rebecca was thirty-one years old; she had three daughters, ages eleven, eight, and three; and she was pregnant. But Rebecca knew she would step up to the challenge. As she would later recall in a written statement made for a court case in 1850, "Necessity is a stern taskmistress and my every want gave me courage, besides I had promised my dying husband I would remain. . ."

Rebecca would not just remain at the mill, she would make it flourish for decades under her leadership, and the mill would be run by her descendants into the late twentieth century. But her path would not be an easy one. Along the way, her strength and fortitude would be tested not only by business issues but by family disputes as well. She would have to fight her family to prove that the Brandywine Iron Works belonged to her, she would have to assume the running of the mill, and she would have to do these things as a woman operating in a man's world.

America was in the midst of the Industrial Revolution, and in 1825 the steel and iron industries were arguably among the most masculine of all industries, since it took great strength to work with iron and the process was hot and dirty. Although Rebecca operated as the mill owner and manager and negotiated contracts for the sale of the iron and the buying of materials, she was greatly served by her brother-in-law, Solomon Lukens, who took over the physical operation of the mill. The mill employed about a dozen workers, and they and their future generations considered the mill part of their family.

Rebecca had made the promise to run the mill to her husband with full knowledge that the task ahead of her would be a daunting one. She knew demand for iron had been low lately, and that she and Charles had laid out a lot of money to repair the equipment at the mill. But not until she reviewed the accounts of the business did she realize the full situation. As she would later recall in her court statement from 1850, "The estate showed an alarming deficiency when the books were examined. I will not dwell on my feelings when I began to look around me; there was difficulty and danger on every side."

The "difficulty and danger" Rebecca referred to was not just of a financial nature. Rebecca's mother was anything but supportive of her daughter's decision to run the mill. In her 1850 court statement, Rebecca wrote that her mother "offered no assistance if I left but thought, as a female, I was not fit to carry on such a concern. I then firmly but most respectfully told her I must make the attempt."

Rebecca and her mother did not share a close relationship; in fact, she had never felt a bond with her. After her husband's death Rebecca wrote an autobiography for her children, and in it she described her relationship with her mother bluntly and honestly by writing, "Between my mother and me there had never been that endearing familiarity which ought to exist between parent and child. She was even reserved, and rather repelled than claimed my confidence."

Rebecca was the first of nine children born to Isaac Pennock and his wife, Martha Webb Pennock. The Pennocks were Quakers, and they lived in Fallowfield in Chester County, Pennsylvania. After farming for a while, Isaac instead decided to build an ironworks, which he called the Federal Slitting Mill. The mill made iron rods and strips that were used for wagon wheels, barrel hoops, and nails. Blacksmiths also bought the iron, which they would then transform into other objects, such as horseshoes. Isaac owned land in addition to the ironworks, and by the time Rebecca was born on January 6, 1794, the Pennocks were well-off financially. As Quakers, Rebecca's parents believed the sexes were equal in ability, and Isaac taught Rebecca to read, write, and do arithmetic. He also took her along with him to his mill. While she wasn't practicing what she had been taught or touring the mill with her father, Rebecca roamed the countryside, riding her horse and enjoying the nature that enveloped her home. Although she interacted often with her father, the same was not true of her mother. In her autobiography, she would recall, "I was the first to name him Father and on me was his affection fondly lavished. My first ideas abound with instances of his endulgence. My mother, occupied with the care of an increasing family, had light control over my actions and I was left to the exercise of my own will in my childish pursuits."

At the age of twelve, Rebecca was sent to boarding school, where she excelled in chemistry and French. Her schooling ended

REBECCA LUKENS

at the age of sixteen and she returned home. By now Rebecca's father was also part-owner of another mill, the Brandywine Iron Works, and the Pennock family had grown to include two brothers and four sisters. The youngest child was placed in Rebecca's care. Although she didn't enjoy her new responsibilities at first, she came to love the child, and the two of them spent many days wandering the hills that surrounded their home. Rebecca often indulged her love of reading while the boy played, and she eventually pleaded with her father for the chance to go back to school. Ever indulgent, Isaac agreed, and Rebecca attended boarding school until 1812.

A few weeks after she arrived home from boarding school, Rebecca traveled to Philadelphia with her father, where she visited with friends. Through one of these acquaintances, whom Rebecca refers to in her autobiography as Mrs. W____., she met her future husband, Charles Lukens. Charles was a Quaker and a physician with a thriving practice in Abington, a town about twelve miles outside Philadelphia, and Rebecca's young heart was awakened to love. But, as she would later relate in her autobiography, since Rebecca was leaving the city in a few days with her father to return home, she " . . . banished, or strove to banish his image from my mind and mixed with my friends the gayest of the gay. My pride assisted me in driving the fascinating form of the stranger from my mind, and in a few days I returned with my father home." Weeks later, in early summer, Charles accompanied Mrs. W____. and her husband on a visit to the Pennocks. After a few days, Charles declared his feelings for Rebecca and asked if he could visit her from time to time. Rebecca assented, and a romance blossomed, culminating in their marriage on March 23, 1813.

After marrying Rebecca, Charles decided to give up his medical practice to become a partner with Rebecca's father in the Federal Slitting Mill, which was now known as the Rokeby Iron Works. The Lukens' first child, Martha, was born in 1814. In 1816 Isaac

Pennock bought out his partner in the Brandywine Iron Works and urged Charles and Rebecca to take charge of the enterprise, which they did. They moved into the house on the farm beside the mill, and Charles took over as ironmaster by leasing the business from Isaac for $420 per year. The couple started to make much-needed repairs to the mill and farmhouse with the understanding that the mill would be left to Rebecca by her father upon his death.

The mill produced iron sheets and rods that were cut into nails, but Charles saw the future potential of rolling the iron. Many businesses were starting to run their machinery on steam from water that was heated in iron boilers, which were made from flat pieces of iron called boilerplate. Charles made changes to the mill, and on December 30, 1818, the Brandywine Iron Works became the first mill in America to roll iron boilerplate; the company was soon also rolling steel boilerplate. By producing larger pieces of metal, less metal needed to be fused together for end products, which meant fewer areas of weakness in the seams where the metal plates met. Brandywine Iron Works would become known for its boilerplate, and its use would increase exponentially during the American Industrial Revolution, when steam-powered locomotives and ships were first being designed.

As the years progressed, Rebecca and Charles added to their family. Another daughter, Elizabeth, was born in 1817. Two sons arrived next, Charles Edward in 1819 and Isaac in 1821. Isaac was not a healthy child, and he died less than a year after his birth. Also in the year 1822, Rebecca gave birth to another daughter, Isabella. Tragedy struck a double blow in 1824 when the death of Rebecca's father was soon followed by the death of Charles Edward.

Although Rebecca was undoubtedly saddened by the death of her sons, her father's death would claim the biggest impact on her life thus far. Although Isaac Pennock had often told Rebecca the Brandywine Iron Works would be hers upon his death, his will did not make this clear. Instead it stated that his property would be appraised and equally divided among his five daughters and his two sons would each receive a farm. Rebecca assumed that the disposition of assets would occur in 1827 when her youngest sister came of age, but she would recall in her court statement made in 1850 that "Mother then startled me by declaring that it was optional with her when the appraisement should be, neither did that weaken her claim to it during her life if she chose to hold it . . ." Her mother also made it clear that when she chose to distribute the estate, no consideration would be given Rebecca for the amount of improvements and payments that Rebecca and Charles had already made on the mill.

Rebecca and Charles no doubt felt uneasy with Martha Pennock in charge, and Charles's sudden death in 1825 complicated matters even further. While Rebecca was grieving for her beloved husband and pregnant with their child, her mother made her life even harder by demanding repayments of business loans that Isaac had made to Charles for the running of the ironworks. With lots of hard work and a bit of good timing, Rebecca was able to meet the debts owed. She would state in her 1850 court statement that ". . . our character for making boiler iron stood first in the market. . . . The first money I ever made was spent in satisfying the claim against the estate of my husband, the rest in paying off my Mother, and few at this day know that, but for my exertion, the estate of Dr. Lukens would have failed to reach the claims against it."

By this time the Brandywine Iron Works was known for its excellent quality of boilerplate. Before his death, Charles had negotiated a deal that provided sheet iron for the hull of the *Codorus,* the first ship with an iron hull to be built in the United States. The year after his death saw the birth of the first steam railroad engine, and under Rebecca's leadership, Brandywine Iron Works began making iron plate for locomotives. Slowly the business began to be financially successful. Five months after her husband's death, Rebecca gave birth to her last child, a daughter who she named Charlesanna in memory of the child's father. Every morning Rebecca left her house and walked the short distance that separated the house from the mill. By having her house so near, she was able to intertwine her business and motherly duties, and she managed both well.

But while Rebecca was working diligently at the mill, it was still not legally her property. In 1827, when Rebecca's youngest sister came of age, Martha Pennock decided she would distribute her late husband's estate. Against Rebecca's objections, her mother included Brandywine Iron Works in the appraisement of the estate. Brandywine was appraised at $11,000, a price that greatly reflected all the improvements made by Rebecca and Charles over the years. As the oldest child, Rebecca was first to choose what estate holdings she wanted, and although she felt she was being charged twice for the improvements to the mill she had made, she chose the ironworks. She had to pay nearly $5,000 to her sisters to make the distribution of the estate equal.

In addition to receiving payment on the balance of the debt Charles had owed Isaac when he died, plus interest on the loan, Martha Pennock also insisted that Rebecca agree to pay her a yearly annuity of $100, probably following a Pennsylvania statute of 1764 that required a child who purchased an estate from a widowed mother to pay an annual rent to ensure the care of the mother. Rebecca's disgust with her mother was clear when she recalled in her 1850 court statement that she told Solomon Lukens, who acted as negotiator between Rebecca and her mother, "I have no right now to pay anything for Brandywine and Mother knows it well, yet if by paying the sum ($100) yearly will bring peace with it I will gladly comply." In the same statement Rebecca estimated that she had paid her mother $14,000 to $15,000 for the mill in the years after her father's death, not including the annuity, which, although she insisted it be set aside for her, Martha Pennock never actually claimed.

With the ownership of Brandywine Iron Works finally resolved, Rebecca and her children settled into an everyday routine. Business in the steel and iron industry was good, and the quality of the boilerplate made at Brandywine was of such high quality that some companies in England also bought it for making railroad engines. The Industrial Revolution was in full swing in America, and transportation by ship and railroad was exploding. Under Rebecca's direction, Brandywine provided iron and steel boilerplates for the many steamboats and steam engines being built at the time. But once again, personal tragedy would foreshadow Rebecca's business fortunes. In 1832 her daughter Elizabeth died at age fifteen, and Rebecca was heartbroken. Rather than withdrawing into herself, Rebecca put all her energy into overhauling the mill and her house. She refurbished both, and she also built houses for the men who worked for her, whom she considered part of her family.

But, as often happens, great expansion in the United States was followed by extreme contraction, and America experienced its worst financial crisis to date, the Panic of 1837. Banks failed, businesses closed, and an economic depression followed. These were definitely some of the hardest financial times for Rebecca and the mill, as evidenced by her letter of May 1837 to Hannah Pennock Steel in which she wrote, "All is paralyzed—business at a stand. I have as yet lost nothing but am in constant fear, and have even forbidden my agents to sell not knowing who would be safe to trust." Many iron and steel mills closed or laid off workers at this time, but Rebecca managed to keep the Brandywine Iron Works afloat without layoffs. When the orders for boilerplate stopped, Rebecca kept the mill workers on the payroll by having them repair machinery and work on aspects of the mill. She also had them work on her farm that adjoined the mill. When money ran out, she gave the workers food from her farm instead of wages.

While Rebecca was seeing her business through the troubled times of the late 1830s, her three daughters were growing up. By all accounts Martha, Isabella, and Charlesanna were happy sisters who shared close relationships with one another and their mother. The oldest daughter, Martha, wed Abraham Gibbons Jr. in 1841, and in 1842 he joined the family firm as superintendent of the mill. Gibbons became a partner in 1844, and the business was renamed Lukens & Gibbons.

Also in 1844, Rebecca's mother died, an event that began another family dispute over Isaac Pennock's estate. At her death, Martha Pennock had five surviving children, but she left her estate to only three of them—her two younger daughters and a son. Martha Pennock cut Rebecca and her sister Martha Coates out of her will. Rebecca and her sister's husband immediately filed an objection because they felt that Isaac Pennock had left his estate to his wife with the understanding that any surplus that was left at her death would be divided equally among their children. This was a complex case in which the court would have to decide if Isaac had left his estate to his wife outright, whereby she could do anything she wanted with it, or whether he had left it to his wife in trust with the understanding that funds left over at her death would go equally to their offspring. The Pennsylvania Supreme Court would review the case three times, in 1845, 1850, and 1853, before deciding that Isaac had willed his estate to his wife, and she could therefore distribute it as she pleased. The Brandywine Iron Works were not part of the legal proceedings, since Rebecca's ownership had been clearly defined in 1827.

Rebecca officially retired from the firm of Lukens & Gibbons in 1847, but she remained a silent partner who retained much influence. The agreement between Rebecca and her eldest daughter's husband stated, "The name and title of the Firm shall be 'A. Gibbons Jr. & Co.' and the affairs and business thereof subject always to the advisement and concurring judgment of the said Rebecca W. Lukens. . . ." The agreement stated that Rebecca would supply two-thirds of the business's capital and Gibbons would supply the other third, and they would share in the profits in the same proportions. Rebecca would also be paid $14,000 per year for rental of the mill and Gibbons would receive $1,000 per year as manager of the mill.

Rebecca's two other daughters had serious suitors whom they would marry the following year. Probably because of all the heartache that she and Charles had endured when they first took over the Brandywine Iron Works from her father, Rebecca made sure her future sons-in-law understood the exact ownership of the firm by having them sign the agreement between her and Gibbons as witnesses.

Isabella married Charles Huston in 1848. In striking similarity to Charles Lukens, Huston gave up his medical practice and joined the family firm as a partner in 1850. Subsequently the name of the company was changed to Gibbons & Huston. Charlesanna also wed a physician, William Tingley, in 1848. Charlesanna became pregnant soon after the nuptials, but she had a difficult pregnancy and died while giving birth to a daughter. On her deathbed Charlesanna asked her mother to raise her child. Rebecca was almost sixty years old, but just as she had agreed to take over the firm when her husband requested it on his deathbed, she once again stepped up and agreed to raise her grandchild.

During the 1850 Supreme Court review of the case concerning Martha Pennock's handling of her husband's estate, Rebecca wrote a statement for the court that detailed her relationship with the Brandywine Iron Works and her family. At the time she was also mourning the death of Charlesanna, and the toll on her came through when she penned, "In this long and weary struggle to gain a living—the estrangement and protracted suit so long pending—the very energies of life seem exhausted."

Probably because of all the legal disputes surrounding Isaac Pennock's estate and holdings, Rebecca was very specific in the will she wrote in 1850, ensuring that her two surviving daughters would share equally in her personal estate and her share of the family business. She also made sure her granddaughter, whom she had named Charlesanna, would be taken care of financially. When Rebecca died of apoplexy four years later, on December 10, 1854, her estate was valued at more than $100,000, an enormous sum at that time.

Her firm, started as the Brandywine Iron Works, would continue as a family business for more than a century. Abraham Gibbons left the firm in 1855 to enter the banking profession, and Charles Huston took over the running of the mill. In 1858 the mill was renamed the Lukens Rolling Mill in honor of Rebecca. When Martha Lukens Gibbons sold her interest in the mill to her sister, Isabella Huston, in 1881, Isabella took an active role in the business just as her mother had.

Two hundred years after her birth, Rebecca Lukens was named the nation's first woman industrial leader by the Pennsylvania Senate. The Lukens Steel Mill, as it would later be called, merged with Bethlehem Steel in 1998 under the name Bethlehem-Lukens Plate. During its lifetime, steel and iron from the mill were used to make ships and trains and also used in other engineering projects, such as the Cooley Dam and the St. Louis Arch.

Rebecca Webb Lukens certainly fulfilled the promise she made to her husband on his deathbed. She took a struggling mill, turned it into a profitable business, and successfully passed it on to future generations of her family.

MARY AMBLER

1805–1868

First Responder

MARY AMBLER STRODE TOWARD where she had heard the loud explosion, clutching the medical supplies she had swiftly gathered from her home before setting out. At fifty-six years of age, Mary knew a noise that loud didn't mean anything good. As she walked along, she caught the distinctive smell of burning wood. After walking about a mile, she could see a huge blaze in the distance.

Mary was making her way to what would later be known as The Great Train Wreck of 1856, the worst railroad disaster in the world up to that time. Around 6:15 a.m. on July 17, 1856, two trains traveling in opposite directions collided head-on near the Wissahickon Station in Montgomery County, Pennsylvania. The Aramingo was a commuter train carrying twenty passengers. The Shakamaxon was an excursion train carrying between 1,000 and 1,500 passengers, mostly children, to Fort Washington, site of a famous Revolutionary War battle and now a park.

When the trains collided, their boilers made contact, and the explosion that resulted was heard five miles away. The first three cars of the Shakamaxon became pieces of smashed wood from the impact, and the train derailed. As it lay on its side, there was an explosion, and the resulting fire could be seen for miles. The blaze spread quickly among the remaining cars. Although people in the crowd that had gathered from neighboring towns wanted to help, no one could get near enough because of the heat of the inferno. A bucket brigade was formed and stretched from the accident site to Sandy Run Creek, twenty-five feet below the railroad tracks. But the brigade was no match for the fire, which raged until the Congress Engine and Hose Company of Chestnut Hill arrived and snuffed it out. It would later be determined that most of the victims died not from the impact but from the terrific fire that ensued after the crash. The *Daily Evening Bulletin* newspaper reported that "the most horrible sight of all was that of the burning cars—for in a few minutes after the collision, the fire spread rapidly through the broken remnants, burning and roasting to death many men, women, and children. The groans and shouts of wounded and those held by the rescuers were of a character to appall the bravest heart."

When Mary Ambler arrived at the terrible wreck, she quickly turned the crowd that had gathered at the scene into an organized relief effort. Realizing no doctors had arrived yet, Mary began administering first aid to the injured with the supplies she had brought with her. Many bodies were charred, and Mary relied on cries of pain to lead her to people who could still be helped. Fifty-nine victims had been killed by the impact and the fire, and there were more than one hundred people injured. Many of the victims were children, which made the relief effort even more gut-wrenching. It was a sweltering July day, but Mary worked nonstop. She was a small woman who never weighed more than one hundred pounds, yet she took charge of the crowd and put them to work in an orderly fashion. She worked among the injured while overseeing the others who were helping. Mary was definitely the leader, and the other volunteers looked to her to say what should be done and when.

There was smoke everywhere, and women and children who had been in the rear cars of the Shakamaxon train and escaped serious injury were also part of the chaos. Many of the women were looking for their older children, who had been riding with the Reverend Daniel Sheridan in the lead car. The reverend was from St. Michael's Roman Catholic Church in the Kensington section of Philadelphia, and he was taking the children in his Sunday school classes on a picnic at Shaeff's Woods, a popular picnic site within Fort Washington. In fact, the excursion train the Sunday school children rode in was called the "picnic special" because so many Philadelphians rode it to Fort Washington to picnic and spend the day relaxing and enjoying the scenery afforded by Fort Washington's location high above the Hudson River.

The calling of names by mothers as they searched for their children was a devastating sound. Even worse was the weeping that could be heard many times as children were found—but not alive. Of the fifty-nine people killed, forty-three were younger than age twenty. The Reverend Sheridan and the engineer of the picnic special were among the dead. Due to the extreme impact of the collision and the ensuing fire, the bodies of many victims were never found, and some of those that were found were never identified because they were burned beyond recognition.

Among the cries of the wounded, those searching for loved ones, and the mourners, Mary Ambler worked calmly and methodically. She did her best to determine who could be tended to easily and who would need more involved medical care. She also kept the local townspeople around her working in a concerted and organized way. As she moved among the hundred or so injured, it became clear to Mary that some would need more care than could be provided at the site of the wreck. She decided her home would serve as a makeshift hospital. When she was asked how the injured were to be moved the two miles to her house, Mary instructed the crowd to take the shutters off nearby houses and use them as stretchers, a brilliant idea that kept the relief effort moving.

Back at her house, Mary tore sheets and petticoats into strips to make bandages for the injured. She worked tirelessly and without complaint for almost twenty-four hours straight. Doctors and nurses arrived eventually to help, but Mary's quick actions in the minutes and hours immediately after the accident no doubt saved many lives. And Mary was dedicated to their full recovery. The injured remained in Mary's house until they were well enough to leave on their own or until family came to get them. During their convalescence, Mary continued to care for patients, who by now were also being treated by doctors, nurses, and the Sisters of Charity, an order of nuns. When the railroad later offered to reimburse Mary for the expenses she incurred while nursing the injured, she declined the offer.

No one who knew Mary was surprised by her selfless actions. Born on March 24, 1805, into a Quaker family of German descent, Mary Johnson always had a generous spirit and a helping hand for anyone in need. She was a devout Quaker who led her life according to her religious principles. Mary married Andrew Ambler on May 14, 1829, and the couple moved in with Andrew's parents in Montgomery Square in Montgomery County. They would remain here until Andrew completed the three-year apprenticeship he was serving under his father, who was in the weaving industry. While here, Mary gave birth to two sons, Joseph in 1830 and Benjamin in 1831.

When Andrew's apprenticeship was complete in 1832, he purchased the Fulling Mill and eighty-three acres that surrounded it. This area of Montgomery County was home to many mills, but most ground grain for food. The Fulling Mill was dedicated to making sheep's wool into blankets and clothing. Andrew was not the first owner of the mill. It had been in operation for a century already and was in terrible shape when Andrew purchased it. The repairs he made were so extensive that by the time he was done working on the mill, it was as if it had been rebuilt.

Mary and Andrew's first home of their own as a wedded couple was located about fifty feet west of the mill, in the oldest home in the area. Over the years Mary gave birth to six more children, for a total of eight offspring. The last child, named Mary, was born in 1848, when her mother was a week away from her forty-third birthday, and she lived only about six weeks. The other children, born between 1830 and 1842, were all boys.

Mary was well known within her community. She opened a Sunday school for area children and ran it in her home, and she was always helping neighbors who fell ill or got hurt. Mary and Andrew owned the only well in the area, and Mary always allowed her neighbors to draw from it when necessary.

At the time of The Great Train Wreck of 1856, Mary Ambler was a widow. Andrew had passed away in 1850, and Mary had taken over running the mill with her older sons. During the Civil War the successful mill manufactured Union uniforms and supplied the army with woolens and blankets. After the train victims were done convalescing, Mary returned to a quiet existence. She passed away on August 18, 1868, and was buried alongside her husband at Gwynedd Friends Meeting.

The Great Train Wreck of 1856 was a defining moment not only in the life of Mary Ambler but also in the evolution of safety protocols within the transportation industry. Wikipedia describes the wreck as "the worst railroad catastrophe in the world until the 1870s, and indeed, one of the single worst events of its time, having an impact that rivals that of September 11, 2001, in the modern era."

In 1856 the North Pennsylvania Railroad Company, which owned the railway connecting Philadelphia with the Lehigh Valley of Montgomery County, was in its infancy. Although the maiden voyage on the line had occurred only a year earlier than the wreck, on

July 2, 1855, the people of the area took a liking to train travel right away. Besides being able to travel places more easily, business owners were thrilled with the increase in sales the railroad afforded them, since they could now ship their products to customers farther away.

Trains were full with people and products, but safety regulations had not kept up with the growth of the industry. There was no communications between trains that would be traveling in opposite directions on the same tracks, so there was no way of communicating that a train was running off its schedule. Instead, engineers on the North Pennsylvania Railroad followed a fifteen-minute rule for train departures in the case of a delayed train: The conductor of the train awaiting the passing of a train in the opposite direction had to wait another fifteen minutes if the oncoming train didn't appear. Also, the conductor of the delayed train was to move his train onto a siding if he couldn't make it to the expected meeting place within that fifteen-minute interval.

The picnic special pulled out of the station in Philadelphia at 5:10 a.m., twenty-three minutes late. The locomotive Shakamaxon was engineered by Henry Harris, and it was known for having problems with its steam pressure—it had to make periodic stops to build up enough steam pressure to continue. Meanwhile, William Vanstavoren, engineer of the Aramingo train, waited at the Wissahickon Station for the excursion train to pass on the single rail the two trains would share. The excursion train was expected at the station at 6:00 a.m., and the local train was scheduled to leave the station in the opposite direction at 6:15 a.m. When the Shakamaxon did not appear by 6:15, Vanstavoren felt he had followed the fifteen-minute rule, and the Aramingo left the station.

Meanwhile, Henry Harris was trying to make up the lost time on the Shakamaxon line. He knew the commuter train Aramingo was scheduled to be coming the opposite direction on the same track, but he felt he could use a siding to allow the train to safely pass him. After all, following the fifteen-minute rule, the Aramingo would not leave the station until fifteen minutes after its schedule, which would mean it would leave at 6:30 a.m.

The fifteen-minute rule was applied by both engineers but in different ways. The engineer of the local train thought he only had to wait fifteen minutes from when the other train was expected, and the engineer of the excursion train thought the Aramingo wouldn't take off for an extra fifteen minutes from its scheduled departure. Because of the differences in the engineers' interpretations, the two trains collided at 6:18 a.m. as each rounded a blind turn.

The accident occurred on a Thursday, and the North Pennsylvania Railroad shut down operations on the following Sunday to honor the victims. The railroad also provided financially for people who were injured and families of those who had died in the wreck. Shares of stock were offered first, and if that wasn't accepted, the railroad made cash payments. There was an inquiry into the cause of the crash, which was witnessed by John Spencer, a local citizen who lived near the site of the collision. He testified, "I was looking out of my shop window and saw the train approaching. I saw the down train first, just coming through the cut above Camp Hill Station. . . . I had just time enough to turn around and saw the up train coming under the bridge at Camp Hill station. . . . "

Eventually it was concluded that Henry Harris, engineer of the excursion train, who had died in the crash, was at fault for what the jury called "gross carelessness." But the verdict came too late for William Vanstavoren, the engineer of the local train. He blamed himself for the crash and committed suicide shortly after the accident.

The railroad industry made wide-reaching changes because of the crash. From the time of the crash onward, the telegraph was used to communicate important messages between stations. Engineers also realized that sounding their train's whistle, which the

Shakamaxon had done continuously, was of no use because the sound did not travel forward.

The crash also had broad implications for protocols in other industries. Lessons learned by systems engineers who studied the reasons for the wreck are applied today to many industries, such as computer software design. When systems engineers decide how to handle right-of-way issues that pertain to data, such as which computer should have priority if there's a conflict, they are applying what was learned from The Great Train Wreck of 1856.

At the time of the train wreck, there were two stations with the name Wissahickon, one of which was located across the lane from where Mary had lived. Railroad officials decided to rename this station a year after Mary Ambler's death, and the townspeople were asked to pick the new name. They came up with four names of founding families or prominent citizens of the area, one of whom was Mary Ambler, the only woman to be nominated. When the townspeople couldn't decide which of the four names should be awarded the honor, the railroad made the decision itself. It changed the name of the Wissahickon station to Ambler on July 20, 1869, to honor all that Mary Ambler had done during The Great Train Wreck of 1856. When the area village decided to incorporate into a borough on November 22, 1887, they decided to adopt the name of the Ambler station, also to honor Mary's actions during one of the worst tragedies in American history.

The town of Ambler, situated about twelve miles northwest of Philadelphia, is still thriving today. The 2000 census listed its population at just more than 6,400 persons. Mary Ambler's home is still standing on Main Street, and it still serves as a family home. The Coach Inn, located just off the Fort Washington exit of the expressway around Ambler, has two railroad cars in the design of those from the mid-nineteenth century and also honors Mary's memory by having her name on the dining car.

ANN PRESTON

1843–1872

Pioneering Doctor

As per their instructions, Dr. Ann Preston and the female medical students entered Pennsylvania Hospital by way of the back stairs. Their backdoor arrival was heralded by a waiting group of male medical students, who hissed, threw wads of paper, and insulted the women. Some of the men even squirted tobacco juice at them. Dr. Preston and her students refused to be intimidated and calmly proceeded to attend their scheduled clinic. After the incident, a meeting was held among representatives from the medical staffs of all the hospitals in Philadelphia. The question put before the group was whether women medical students should be allowed to participate in the medical clinics that male physicians in training regularly attended at Philadelphia hospitals. The answer was a resounding no.

But Ann Preston, dean of the Woman's Medical College of Pennsylvania, was not about to accept defeat. Although her students attended clinics at the Woman's Hospital of Philadelphia, which Ann had founded in 1861, she did not want their education limited only to female patients or female-related issues. By using the press to sway public opinion in her favor, Ann was eventually able to get

Philadelphia hospitals to open their *front* doors to women physicians in training. They were not welcomed with open arms, and the female students often had to endure harassment, but because of Ann's perseverance the sight of women participating in clinics alongside men became less and less of a novelty.

This was not the first time Ann had played a pivotal role in the battle she and other women of her time waged to be accepted in the medical profession. When Dr. Preston and her students entered Pennsylvania Hospital in 1869, women had already come a long way since Elizabeth Blackwell had been the first woman to graduate from an American medical school twenty years earlier. Medicine itself had come a long way—in 1800 only two hospitals existed in the United States, and the stethoscope was not yet invented. Most surgeries were undertaken to treat wounds or repair broken bones, and textbooks on the subject devoted the most space to showing how to perform amputations. Practicing medicine in the United States didn't require a license, and treatment options were as varied as the physicians who promoted them. Homeopathic cures were commonly prescribed, as were magnetic, electrical, and steam treatments.

By the mid–1800s medical schools had been established in America, but there were no academic standards that determined enrollment eligibility. A formal education was not needed for a student to be accepted, although students were expected to know enough Latin to write prescriptions. The only formal preparation required by a student was to study under a practicing physician for a year. Once accepted by a school, the student was required to spend a four-month period attending seven courses of lectures given by practicing physicians. The next year the student would attend the same courses again and write a thesis. Passing an oral examination was the culmination of the student's education.

But as women began applying to medical schools, they discovered there was an additional entrance requirement—you had to be a male. Women applicants were routinely turned away. Elizabeth Blackwell was the first woman accepted at an American medical school, and her triumph was a fluke. When Elizabeth's application arrived in 1847 at Geneva Medical College at Geneva, New York, the administration decided to put the question of her admittance before the students of the school. The students voted for her to be admitted—because they thought her application was a practical joke. Even after the first hurdle of acceptance was overcome, Elizabeth had to fight to be able to attend all the classes offered, even those some of her teachers thought were inappropriate for a woman. Despite the adversities she faced, Elizabeth graduated in January 1849 at the top of her class, becoming America's first woman to earn a medical degree.

Unlike Elizabeth, most women who aspired to be doctors found the doors to American medical schools firmly shut. The future of women in American medicine was secured only when a group of Quakers established the first medical school for women. They built their school in Philadelphia and named it the Female Medical College of Pennsylvania. Social reformer Lucretia Mott was the catalyst responsible for the school coming into being. After being impressed with some women medical students she met at the first public health lectures given in Philadelphia, Lucretia convinced local businessman William Mullen of the need for the school. Lucretia and William and their spouses formed a partnership with four doctors, raised the money needed, and opened the doors to the school in 1850.

Ann Preston was one of the first students to apply for admission. She was in her mid-thirties and had already apprenticed under a physician for two years. Her age was not a concern; many women came to the field of medicine after teaching, raising families, or otherwise tending to the needs of others. By the time of her enrollment, Ann had already buried her mother and two sisters, which had resulted in her inheriting the woman's role of running her father's household and caring for her six brothers.

ANN PRESTON

Born on December 1, 1813, Ann was the second child and the first girl born to Amos and Margaret Preston, Quakers who resided in West Grove, a village about thirty-five miles from Philadelphia that grew up around a Friends Meeting House that had been built in 1787. Amos Preston was a Quaker minister, and he and his wife instilled religious teachings in their children. Ann grew up surrounded by a loving family who believed in the Quaker principles of equality, simplicity, and pacifism. The family put their beliefs into action in their everyday lives, and the Preston home served as a stop on the Underground Railroad, the system by which runaway slaves traveled to freedom in the north. One time when Ann was just a child, her quick thinking saved a runaway slave hiding in their house from being caught by slave hunters who were searching nearby properties. She quickly dressed the slave in her mother's plain dress, bonnet, and gloves, and when the slave hunters arrived, Ann and the slave calmly walked past them. The two appeared to be heading to a Quaker meeting, and the slave hunters were fooled. Following the Quaker belief that taught her not to engage in any frivolous activities, Ann was a serious child who spent her time in the pursuit of bettering herself. She attended a Quaker school in her small hometown and then attended a Quaker boarding school in the town of West Chester, about fifteen miles from West Grove. When her mother became ill, Ann was called home to care for her. Besides caring for her mother, Ann also took care of her six brothers, her father, and her sister. One of Ann's sisters had already passed away, and Ann's mother and remaining sister would also succumb to the illnesses that plagued them.

While many young people might have been overcome by sadness, or been exhausted by caring for a father and six younger brothers, Ann remained a cheerful person involved in her community. The local literary association and lyceum sponsored public lectures, and Ann continued her education by attending as many as time allowed.

She was also involved in the temperance and antislavery movements that were gaining momentum in the United States, even writing some petitions and lectures for the Clarkson Anti-Slavery Society.

Once her brothers were old enough to take care of themselves, Ann decided to become a teacher. She had learned through experience how society treated men and women very differently, even within her Quaker community, which believed in the equality of all people. Although women in West Grove were not treated as inferior beings, they still held traditional roles that resulted in most of their time being spent indoors cooking, cleaning, and caring for the family. Women dressed in tightly bound clothing as they performed their household duties, while men predominantly wore looser fitting clothes and worked outdoors. Ann decided that women should be taught more about how their bodies worked, so after spending time studying the subject, she started teaching classes on physiology and hygiene to the girls and women in her community. Her teaching sparked an interest in medicine, and in 1847 Ann began working as an apprentice to Dr. Nathaniel Moseley.

Two years later Ann completed her training with Dr. Moseley and applied to four medical colleges in Philadelphia. All of them turned her down because of her gender. Ann was beginning to think her dream of becoming a doctor would remain only that, but then the Pennsylvania legislature passed an act incorporating the Female Medical College of Pennsylvania on March 11, 1850. Ann was one of the first women to apply, and she was in attendance when the private school opened in October 1850.

The Female Medical College of Pennsylvania faced considerable opposition, not only because it would train women to be doctors but also because alternative medicine would be taught. One of the school's founders, Dr. Joseph Longshore, was a homeopathic doctor who firmly believed in the water cure and mesmerism, and many of the faculty shared his beliefs. But when the school opened, many alternative approaches were losing favor as the medical profession became more regulated, especially since the formation of the American Medical Association in 1846. Dr. Longshore resigned in 1853 because he felt the school's teachings were becoming too mainstream; by 1860 the school taught only what was considered "regular" medicine.

The teaching of alternative medicine was not unique to the Female Medical College of Pennsylvania, and there were many more objectors concerned about the gender of the student population than the school's curriculum. Detractors claimed female doctors wouldn't be able to handle the harsh realities of medicine, such as having to recommend surgery or painful procedures, and many felt women could not maintain the cool detachment that was felt necessary to the profession. Always central to the case against female doctors was the prevalent prejudice in society that portrayed women as emotionally and physically weak and intellectually inferior to men.

Ann Preston and the other seven women who made up the first class of the Female Medical College of Pennsylvania persevered through all the controversy. Although the graduation ceremony was marred by male protesters, the graduates received their degrees in December 1851. Ann returned to the college the next year for postgraduate studies and was asked to join the faculty in 1853 as a professor of physiology and hygiene, a position she readily accepted. She spent the next years teaching, giving public lectures on medicine, and establishing her practice. She also began in earnest her fight for equality between male and female doctors.

Male and female physicians held the same medical degrees, but in reality the women were still considered second-class doctors by most of society. Most male doctors would have nothing to do with them, pharmacists would sometimes refuse to fill their prescriptions, and hospitals didn't allow them to treat patients. Many female doctors focused on treating the poor in part because they were the ones who allowed the women to treat them. Rather than the prejudice ebbing, it gained fervor, and in 1858 the Philadelphia Medical Society barred women from educational clinics and medical societies.

In response, Ann organized an all-women board whose goal was to establish a woman's hospital in Philadelphia that would help poor women and give women doctors in training clinical experience. Realizing the Female Medical College of Pennsylvania didn't have enough room on its grounds for a hospital wing to be added, Ann found an appropriate site in the northern part of the city, across from Girard College. She then took on the formidable job of fundraising, walking door to door and describing what she hoped to do and asking for donations.

Three years after Ann began her fund-raising efforts, the Civil War broke out. Ann refused to give up on her endeavor, even after the Female Medical College was forced to close its doors. She continued to raise money by traveling from farm to farm in her buggy and pleading her cause until her financial goal had been reached. The Woman's Hospital of Philadelphia was established in 1861 and opened its doors in 1862. Also in 1862, Ann persuaded the college's board to reopen the school by renting rooms at the new hospital location. Through Ann's efforts, women were finally able to obtain a medical education that included both a classroom and a clinical experience, something that male students had been enjoying for decades.

Ann was appointed to the board of the Woman's Hospital of Pennsylvania, and she resumed teaching at the college when it reopened. In 1863 she expanded the scope of her achievements by opening one of the first nursing schools in the nation at the college and hospital location. Ann reached another milestone when she was named the first female dean at the Female Medical College in 1866. The following year the college changed its name to the Women's Medical College of Pennsylvania, and Ann was appointed to the college's board.

Women were making great strides in medicine, but their services were still limited mostly to treating only women and children. Men were still not welcoming women into the profession. In 1867 the Philadelphia County Medical Society adopted a resolution that disapproved of women in medicine. Ann wrote a superb reply that rebutted every objection the society had voiced and refused to give up fighting for her students to be treated as equals to men. Ann's new fight was to win women medical students the right to attend clinics at all the medical colleges in the area, not just at the Woman's Hospital of Philadelphia. That way, Ann reasoned, they would gain a more diverse knowledge of different medical ailments and treatments. Although she and her students had to endure harassment from male students when they attended a clinic at the Pennsylvania Hospital in 1869, Ann won the battle. Women doctors eventually became an accepted sight at Philadelphia hospitals.

During her tenure as dean at the college, Ann witnessed many historic events. In 1867 the college awarded its first medical degree to an African-American woman, Rebecca J. Cole, who was the second African-American woman to become a doctor in the United States. In 1869 Clara Swain graduated and was the first woman medical missionary to travel to India.

Ann suffered from articular rheumatism and in 1869 was forced to limit her private practice to office visits because it was too hard for her to travel around the countryside to see her patients. She still taught at the college and worked as a consulting physician at the hospital. Ann suffered another acute attack in 1871 from which she never fully recovered, and she passed away on April 18, 1872.

Even in death Ann Preston continued to promote the education of women by instructing that her life savings be used to create a scholarship at the Woman's Medical College of Pennsylvania. The college remained an all-female school until 1970, when financial pressures resulted in the admission of men and the school's name was changed to the Medical College of Pennsylvania.

ELIZABETH THORN

1832-1907

Civil War Caretaker

ELIZABETH THORN LOOKED UP FROM HER WORK, exhausted. She leaned on her shovel and called to her father that it was time to finish up for the day. As she gathered her tools, she adjusted the cloth rubbed with peppermint that she kept under her nose to mask the stench of death. All around her lay the aftermath of battle—dead soldiers, dead horses, blood-soaked ground. The smell of death was everywhere. She had heard that the foul odor permeated the air as far away as Harrisburg, almost fifty miles from where Elizabeth stood looking over the newly turned ground within Evergreen Cemetery. It was July 1863, and Elizabeth and her family had been witness to one of the defining battles of the Civil War—the Battle of Gettysburg. Although the battle had lasted only three days, Elizabeth and other townspeople of Gettysburg would spend months recovering from the ravages of war that were inflicted upon their lives, their homes, and their lands.

Eventually the fame of the pivotal Battle of Gettysburg would grow, and the National Cemetery would be created to dedicate the Union soldiers who fell in combat there. On November 19, 1863,

President Abraham Lincoln would attend the dedication, and his few remarks, forever after known as Lincoln's Gettysburg Address, would ensure the town and its battlefield its rightful place in history. But as Elizabeth glanced down at her day's work within Evergreen Cemetery, all she knew was that her town and her home were in shambles. So many dead men and horses littered the ground you could walk across the field where the Confederates had made their final charge without your feet ever touching the blood-soaked earth.

Elizabeth had already experienced profound changes in her life over the last thirty-one years. Born in Germany in 1832, Elizabeth Masser had sailed to America with her parents in 1854. Not much is known about her life before she came to America, or why she and her parents decided to make Gettysburg their home. After settling in Gettysburg, Elizabeth met another German immigrant, Peter Thorn, and in September 1855 she and Peter were wed.

The newlyweds were aware of the anti-immigrant sentiment that was sweeping the American nation during this time, and eventually it visited their town. Although Gettysburg had been settled by Irish and German immigrants in 1734, by the 1850s some in the succeeding generations felt America's great resources should be reserved for those who had been born in the country. An article in the Gettysburg paper *Star and Banner,* written by the editor of the paper, said Gettysburg would be better off if there were no people born outside the United States within the borough. And in November 1855, just two months after Elizabeth and Peter wed, the American Party staged a political rally in town. Few foreigners had not heard of the American Party. Their goal was to restrict the rights of foreign-born citizens, and banners at the rally declared their platform succinctly by declaring "Americans must rule America," and "We want no European paupers or felons." The Thorns also knew that of all foreigners, German Americans such as themselves were the most likely to be the targets of antiforeigner scorn, so they lived quietly and tried not to draw attention to themselves.

In the mid-1850s, 90 percent of the people living in the town of Gettysburg had been born in America. Anyone with an accent immediately stood out, and no doubt Elizabeth and Peter certainly felt the disdain of many of the town's elite. But the Thorns seem to have been accepted to some degree by their native-born neighbors, as evidenced by Peter being appointed the first caretaker of Evergreen Cemetery in February 1856. By coincidence, Elizabeth and Peter had been married on the day the cornerstone for the cemetery gatehouse had been laid. His annual salary was $150, and caretaker duties included digging graves, burying the deceased, arranging the removal and reburial of remains from other cemeteries, and general cemetery upkeep. The salary also allowed the caretaker and his family to live in the cemetery gatehouse rent-free. By all accounts, Elizabeth and Peter lived quietly, worked hard, and raised their family, which at the time of the battle had grown to include three sons ages six, four, and two, and a fourth child on the way. Elizabeth's parents, who were now in their sixties, also lived at the gatehouse.

Peter joined the Union ranks in the 138th Pennsylvania Infantry in August 1862, and Elizabeth took over his job of caretaker with the help of her father. Before the Battle of Gettysburg, Elizabeth had buried about five people each month. After the battle she and her father would dig more than one hundred graves. And thirty-one-year-old Elizabeth would do much of the backbreaking work while six months pregnant.

The Battle of Gettysburg was fought from July 1 to July 3, but Confederate soldiers first entered the town of Gettysburg on June 26. Elizabeth encountered the Confederates when, as she would later recall in her memoir published in the *Gettysburg Times* on July 2, 1938, six cavalrymen came up the Baltimore Pike "with their

STATUE OF ELIZABETH THORN

revolvers blaring." Elizabeth fainted from fright when they rode into Evergreen Cemetery, as she was "a piece away from the house" and thought that her mother might have been fired on. When she made her way to the gatehouse, the soldiers told her not to be afraid of them, that they weren't going to hurt them, "like the yankees [sic] did their ladies." The Confederates asked for bread and butter and buttermilk, and Elizabeth's mother gathered the food.

Even though she must have been very scared, Elizabeth kept her wits about her. She saw to it that the Confederates were fed and hoped they would soon be on their way. Although she didn't realize the magnitude of death the battle would bring to her town, she did hear firsthand about the demise of one of the first casualties of the Gettysburg campaign, George Sandoe. Elizabeth recorded in her memoir that while the soldiers were resting at the gatehouse eating the food Elizabeth's mother had provided

> . . . a rebel rode up the pike and had another horse beside his. The ones who were eating said to him: "Oh, you have another one." and the one who came up the pike said: "yes, the — — shot at me, but he did not hit me, and I shot at him and blowed him down like nothing, and here I got his horse and he lays down the pike."

The man the Confederate had killed was Sandoe, who had been part of a company in Gettysburg.

The Confederates occupied Gettysburg, and Elizabeth's experience was similar to that of many of the town's women. In her newspaper-published memoir, she recalled:

> We were trying to feed them all we could. I had baked in the morning and had the bread in the oven. They were hungry and smelled the bread. I took a butcher knife and stood before the

oven and cut this hot bread for them as fast as I could. When I had six loaves cut up I said I would have to keep one loaf for my family, but as they still begged for more I cut up every loaf for them.

We had all the glasses and tins and cups and tubs and everything outside filled with water. All the time our little boys were pumping and carrying water to fill the tubs. They handed water to the soldiers and worked and helped this way until their poor little hands were blistered, and their bread I had given away on Friday.

Nobody felt like work any more, and on Wednesday morning they came with big forces, and the battle begun above Gettysburg, near the Springs Hotel on the Ridge in the morning early on Wednesday.

After the actual battle commenced on Wednesday, July 1, the cemetery and gatehouse land were eventually occupied by Union forces under the command of General Howard. When the Union forces came to the gatehouse, one of General Howard's soldiers wanted a man to accompany him on reconnaissance. Elizabeth offered to go along instead, since she felt her father was too old and a thirteen-year-old boy who was among the citizens who had gathered at the house was too young. The memoir published in the *Gettysburg Times* recalled her calm courage.

He refused at first, but I thought there was danger all around, and said I wasn't afraid so he said "Come on."

We walked through flax, and then through a piece of oats, and then we stood in a wheat field. They all held against me coming through the field, but as he said I was all right, and it did not matter, why they gave three cheers and the band played a little piece, and then I walked a little past a tree to where I could see the two roads. I showed him the Harrisburg Road, the York Pike, and the Hunterstown Road.

After Elizabeth pointed out the local roads to the soldier, which were the main north-south and east-west routes through town, she was taken back to the gatehouse, where a soldier in General Howard's command requested that she make supper for the general. Although she had given all her bread away to Confederate soldiers that morning, she managed to make cakes, which she later served to Generals Howard, Sickles, and Slocum. As the generals finished their meal, Elizabeth asked General Howard if he felt she and her family should flee the house. He advised her to stay at the house and told her to pack her best things, which he would have some of his men move to the cellar, where he also told the family they should head to around four o'clock the next morning, as that was when the fighting would begin. Before he left, General Howard gave Elizabeth one more bit of advice, which Elizabeth recorded in her memoir: "When I give you orders to leave the house, don't study about it, but go right away."

Elizabeth and sixteen other civilians, including her parents and three young sons, were in the cellar early the next morning, and they could hear the cannons firing above them. After a few hours, the door to the cellar flew open and a soldier announced that the family was commanded by General Howard to leave the house and get as far away as they could in ten minutes' time. He added that they were to take nothing up but the children and go immediately.

Following the directions of the soldiers around the house, the civilians hurried down the Baltimore Pike and traveled for about a mile and a half before becoming too tired and weak from hunger to go on. They later took refuge at a nearby farmhouse. Near midnight on that first day of the battle, Elizabeth and her father decided to travel home to the gatehouse to check on their belongings and tend to the hogs they owned. They were able to reach the stables, where they discovered their hogs were gone, but they couldn't get near the house because of the number of wounded and dead men who were lying everywhere. The soldiers had been brought there after the fighting of that first day, and the house was now being used as a hospital and as headquarters for General Howard. They had a soldier take them to the cellar, where they found six wounded men; all their belongings except for Elizabeth's mother's shawl were gone. The material loss did not greatly affect Elizabeth, but witnessing the men's suffering did. Elizabeth recalled in her memoir that "the poor wounded men were crying and going on so that we did not want anything then. They called their wives and children to come and wet their tongues." Elizabeth and her father retraced their route back down the Baltimore Pike to the farmhouse, where they gathered the rest of the family and proceeded farther down the pike to another farmhouse. Here Elizabeth baked bread for the troops and her family at night and tended to the sick and wounded soldiers who filled the house. The horrors she witnessed would stay with her forever, and she would later recall in her published memoir, "They had there a big wagon shed where they brought the wounded and took off their limbs, and threw them into the corn crib, and when they had a two horse load they hauled them away."

The family stayed down in the country until four days after the Battle of Gettysburg, heading home on July 7. On the way up the pike, the group ran into David McConaughy, president of the cemetery. Elizabeth would later write that he told her, "Hurry on home, there is more work for you than you are able to do."

When they reached the house, the scene that awaited them was horrific. Every window of the house was bereft of glass, some of the frames were knocked beside the pump shed, and the water pump was no longer working. In the cellar, where all their belongings had been left, Elizabeth found only three featherbeds, which were so full of blood and mud it took Elizabeth and three other women four days of washing to get them clean.

Elizabeth and the rest of the townspeople except for one, Jennie Wade, had survived the Battle of Gettysburg, but the carnage left behind in the town was of epic magnitude. The bodies of dead horses and men were strewn everywhere, and the stench of rotting flesh was as devastating as the visual horror that confronted them. The smell permeated the air from July until the first frost, and locals put peppermint oil under their noses to cover the odor as they cleaned up their town.

Although Elizabeth had helped the Union forces, fled from her home, and tended to sick and dying soldiers, her toughest job was still before her. Elizabeth recorded in her memoir that soon after she returned to the gatehouse, she received a note from David McConaughy saying, "Mrs. Thorn, it is made out that we will bury the soldiers in our Cemetery for a while, so you go for that piece of ground and commence sticking off lots and graves as fast as you can make them."

As caretaker during her husband's absence, Elizabeth had performed all of his duties, including digging graves with the help of her father, despite her pregnancy. As Elizabeth now surveyed the area around the gatehouse, she noted there were fifteen dead horses beside the cemetery and nineteen dead horses in the adjoining field. There were also dead soldiers buried beside the pumphouse, whose bodies would need to be moved. The digging commenced.

Elizabeth would later recall in her memoir, "Well, you may know how I felt, my husband in the army, my father an aged man. Yet for all the foul air we two started in, I stuck off the graves and while my father finished one, I had another one started."

After many days Elizabeth received permission to telegraph some friends to come and help with the enormous job. Two men came to help, but both ended up becoming ill and unable to work, so Elizabeth paid them for their service and carried on with only her father helping her.

Within two weeks of the battle, Elizabeth and her aged father had dug forty graves. They would eventually bury around one hundred men before the National Cemetery, which was dedicated on November 19, 1863, was ready. When Elizabeth gave birth to a baby girl, she named her Rose Meade Thorn in honor of General Meade, the commander of the Army of the Potomac. Unfortunately Rose was not healthy, and she died at a young age. The ordeal of those days weighed on Elizabeth, who later wrote ". . . and from that time on my health failed and for years I was a very sickly woman. In my older days my health has been better, but those hard days have always told on my life."

Elizabeth continued as caretaker of the cemetery until 1865, when Peter Thorn returned from war after witnessing the surrender of Robert E. Lee's troops at Appomattox. They stayed at Evergreen Cemetery until Peter's resignation in 1874, and Elizabeth died a few months after Peter's passing in 1907. Today a statue fifty feet southwest of the cemetery gatehouse commemorates the contributions that Elizabeth Thorn and other townswomen made during and after the Battle of Gettysburg. The *Civil War Women's Memorial,* a seven-foot bronze statue created by renowned Civil War sculptor Ron Tunison, depicts a six-month-pregnant Elizabeth Thorn leaning on a shovel as she rests from her work of burying the battle casualties.

AMANDA BERRY SMITH

1837-1915

Traveling Evangelist

AMANDA BERRY SMITH ENTERED THE Green Street Methodist Episcopal Church and took a seat in the back pew. This was not the church she normally attended, and she nervously glanced about as she waited for John Inskip, the church's pastor, to begin preaching. Amanda hoped his sermon would show her the way to sanctification, a state in which her soul would be pure and she would find total salvation in God. She had been searching for sanctification since she had become a Christian in 1856, more than a decade earlier, and she longed for the peace of mind she felt this state of holiness would bring her. She had spoken to pastors within her own church, but their words had failed to help her achieve sanctification. So she had walked a mile from her home, passing her own church after walking only two blocks along the way, in order to hear Inskip speak.

A large man, John Inskip's voice filled the church as he explained that the state of sanctification (having a pure soul) was attained by having faith. He himself had been sanctified in 1864, and he preached that once a person achieved sanctification through faith, God would sustain the person's holiness in the same way as the person breathed without conscious thought. This explanation made sense to Amanda, and she felt God finally granted her the sanctification she had searched for. In religious fervor, Amanda shouted "Glory to Jesus!"

As soon as the words left her mouth, Amanda held her breath, shocked that she had drawn attention to herself. Amanda was sure every person present knew it was she who had yelled out, not only because she was a stranger but also because she was the only African American sitting among the white congregation of the Green Street Methodist Episcopal Church. She had been so filled with joy she had forgotten that parishioners at white churches sat with their hands folded and listened politely to sermons; they did not shout out and express themselves as people in her African Methodist Episcopal (AME) Church did. She was immensely relieved when John Inskip answered her outburst with "Amen, Glory to God."

Amanda was overjoyed as she left the church, and she excitedly told acquaintances she met on her walk home that the Lord had sanctified her soul. She felt as though she wanted to tell the whole world about God and his ability to purify a person's soul. Eventually Amanda would travel four continents while spreading her message, bringing Christian teachings to people in America, Asia, Africa, and Europe. It would be prophetic that she had achieved sanctification as she sat among the white congregation of the Green Street Methodist Episcopal Church, for much of her preaching would be done in front of predominantly white audiences. She would gain renown as a leader of the Holiness Movement at a time of bitter segregation in the United States, and her accomplishments would loom even larger because Amanda had begun her life as a slave.

Amanda was born in Baltimore County, Maryland, on January 23, 1837, to Sam and Miriam Berry. Sam and Miriam were slaves who had different owners, so they lived on separate farms even though they were married. Sam worked in fields beside his owner, Luke Ensor, and drove produce to market in Baltimore. While in

AMANDA SMITH

Baltimore, he would sell brooms that he stayed up at night making so he could buy his and his family's freedom. Miriam lived on a nearby dairy farm owned by the Green family, one of the largest slave-owning families in the area. Sam eventually was able to buy his freedom, but the Greens refused to allow him to buy freedom for his family.

Amanda was treated well by the Greens, especially by Rachel, the matriarch of the family, but her parents worried that Amanda and her older brother would likely be included in the dowry of one of the Greens's daughters. To their great relief, Rachel Green agreed to the deathbed request made by one of her daughters to free the Berrys, and Amanda and her family, which now included another brother and a sister, were living as free African Americans on Luke Ensor's land in 1840. They had their own small house; their own chickens, pigs, and turkeys; and their own garden.

Ironically, Amanda would learn more about racial prejudice as a free girl than she ever had as a slave. At that time in Maryland, as more and more African Americans were being freed, there were many laws enacted that dictated rules for "free" African Americans. For instance, if an African-American man couldn't prove he could pay his own way, he could be sold into slavery for the rest of the year; African-American farmers weren't allowed to sell certain items, such as corn, wheat, oats, rye, or tobacco, without obtaining licenses that had to be renewed each year; and African Americans couldn't hold a meeting without having whites there to supervise their activities. Free African Americans also could not testify against whites in court or serve on juries, and they weren't allowed to vote. African Americans also were restricted in their travel. A free black had to obtain written permission from a white sponsor to travel out of state, and then the "free" person could not stay out of the state for more than ten days. If a free African American broke any law, reenslavement was always a possibility.

When Amanda's father went to visit his brother in Pennsylvania and failed to return to Maryland within ten days, he broke the law. Technically he had lost his residence status in the state and could legally be sold into slavery. Although Sam Berry was respected by the white families of the area, his flouting of the law concerned some of them, mostly because they felt that if Sam was allowed to do so, then other freed blacks might follow his example. Soon area farmers were dropping by daily to see if Sam had come home yet. Although she was young, about seven or eight years of age, Amanda understood why her mother spent her days crying and watching out the window for her father. The same day her father arrived home, the family left Maryland and moved to the state of Pennsylvania, where Amanda would spend the next twenty years of her life.

Pennsylvania had officially abolished slavery in 1780, and although slavery in the state was ended gradually over time, restrictions placed on free blacks were lifted immediately. When Amanda and her family fled Maryland in 1845 and moved to Shrewsbury Township in York County, Pennsylvania, only the rights to vote and serve in the state militia were withheld from free blacks. York County was one of six Pennsylvania counties adjacent to the Maryland border where free blacks concentrated, and it was a hub for the Underground Railroad, the system by which fugitive slaves traveled north to freedom.

The Berrys settled on a farm owned by John Lowe, a wealthy farmer who employed Amanda's father and brothers as farm laborers and Amanda and her mother as domestics. By 1850 Amanda had eight siblings, and her family of eleven was among the forty-two African Americans who then lived in Shrewsbury Township. While they lived on the Lowe farm, the Berrys' house functioned as a stop on the Underground Railroad. Amanda's father often worked all day farming the fields and then spent the night taking fugitives to the next stop on the Railroad.

Once, slave hunters broke into Amanda's house looking for escaped slaves. They beat her father and generally terrorized the family. After the incident Amanda watched as her mother bravely denounced slavery and those who owned slaves while prominently standing on a platform in the nearby town of New Market. When she left the platform she fearlessly walked right by a bloodhound that was used to catch runaway slaves, and Amanda was inspired by her courage. Another time Luke Ensor had traveled to their house from Maryland looking for a runaway slave who Amanda's parents happened to be hiding. The couple stood up to her father's former owner and prevented the fugitive from being found.

But the Berrys still experienced incidents of prejudice in Shrewsbury. When she was thirteen, Amanda and her older brother tried to attend the school that was about five miles from their house. It was wintertime, and the children endured the harsh weather during their walk, only to be told upon arrival that they would have to wait until the teacher taught the white children. Then, if the teacher had time, she would teach them. After two weeks it was decided that Amanda and her brother would be taught at home by her parents, who were both able to read and write.

A similar situation occurred when Amanda joined the Methodist Church in Shrewsbury. She was the first African American to join the church and attend classes, but since the teacher would teach her only after teaching the rest of the class, Amanda was soon forced to quit. Having to stay so long at church made her late getting Sunday dinner ready, one of her duties as part of her new job as a live-in maid, and she didn't want to risk being fired. Amanda was thirteen, and she wouldn't give the state of her soul much attention again until she almost died at the age of eighteen.

At the time she became ill, Amanda was living in the town of Columbia, in Pennsylvania's Lancaster County, with her husband, Calvin Devine. She had married Calvin in 1854 at the age of seventeen, and the young couple shared a rocky relationship. Unfortunately Amanda realized after her wedding that Calvin drank too much and too often, and he was not a nice person while drunk. To add to their marital troubles, their first child died. They had one other child, a girl they named Mazie.

In 1855 Amanda became deathly ill, and her father traveled from Wrightsville, Pennsylvania, where he then lived, to visit her. While there he asked Amanda to pray with him, and she did, even though she didn't care much about the state of her soul. After they prayed, Amanda fell asleep and dreamed she was at a camp meeting, religious gatherings that had become popular at the time. In her dream Amanda saw herself teaching at the meeting, and when she awoke she decided she would convert to Christianity. She planned to do this quietly and at her own pace. It would take her two years to find the inner peace she longed for, and her conversion to Christianity would take place in the basement of the home she was working in at the time.

On Tuesday, March 17, 1856, Amanda was desperate to be converted. She had been reading her Bible, fasting, and praying for conversion earnestly since the beginning of the year, and she decided that this day she would find the strength to truly believe in God. The moment of conversion finally happened when she went to the cellar and prayed on her knees for God to help her believe in him.

She was devout in her new religious awakening, finding time to pray, take religious classes, and visit the sick; but Amanda still felt something was missing. She sometimes preached at her local church, and her words convinced some to be converted to Christianity, but Amanda was still searching for the second religious experience that she heard some other Christians had achieved. This "second blessing," as many church leaders called it, happened when God cleansed one's soul of sin so the person's life could be fully dedicated to God.

Amanda's search for the second blessing of God was interrupted by the harsh realities that came with the outbreak of the Civil War. Once African Americans were allowed to join the Union forces, Amanda's husband volunteered. He headed south to fight and was a casualty of the war. The southeastern counties where most African Americans in Pennsylvania, including Amanda, resided were close to Southern territory, and there was constant fear that the Confederates would attack. Amanda had obtained a position as a live-in maid with a well-to-do family in Lancaster. When Confederate troops overran Gettysburg in 1863, Amanda was afraid they would continue on to nearby Lancaster.

Amanda fled to Philadelphia, found another position and joined the Mother Bethel African Methodist Church, where she eventually met and married her second husband, James Smith. When they met, Amanda was a widow with a young daughter about nine years of age; James, twenty years older, was also a widower. Although James worked as a waiter, he led Amanda to believe he wanted to be ordained as a preacher. When Amanda agreed to marry him, she envisioned spending her married life as a respected woman who led prayer meetings and visited the sick in her role as a preacher's wife. Shortly after they were married, James confessed that he really did not want to be a preacher but had only told her that so she would marry him. Although Amanda did her best to forgive him, her trust in him was shaken. When James wanted to move to New York in 1865 to take advantage of the post–Civil War financial boom the city was experiencing, Amanda reluctantly agreed.

New York was not kind to the Smiths. When James, Amanda, and Amanda's daughter, Mazie, arrived, they found the city to be dirty and overcrowded. James had secured a job as a waiter at a hotel before they moved, but the position didn't pay enough to allow the family to live together. James lived at the hotel, and Amanda went to work as a live-in maid.

Amanda was lonely and missed her family and friends in Philadelphia, but things really took a turn for the worse when she lost her job once her pregnancy began to show. Amanda's only choice was to move to a charity shelter, where she stayed a week. Luckily a couple James had known in Philadelphia let Amanda move in with them, where she stayed until she gave birth on September 16, 1866, to a boy she named Thomas Henry Smith.

Three weeks after Thomas's birth, Amanda secured a live-in maid position and moved into her own apartment, a damp basement room at 135 Amity Street in Greenwich Village. Here she sustained herself and her children by hiring herself out as a day cleaner and taking in laundry; James helped her pay her rent, although they lived separately.

The death of Thomas from meningitis when he was only eight months old strained Amanda's already unsteady marriage, but she gave birth to another boy, who they named William Henry Smith, on August 1, 1868. James found a job as a coachman that provided living quarters for him and his family, but when he asked Amanda to move from Greenwich Village to New Utrecht to be with him, she hesitated. His new position was in the country, and Amanda had just finally gotten used to her neighborhood and begun to have regular customers in her laundry business. She told James that she needed until the following spring to decide whether she wanted to give up the security she finally felt she had, and James moved to his new position without his wife and family. It was during this time that Amanda had once again begun seeking sanctification, a journey that met with success that fateful Sunday in September 1868 when she heard John Inskip preach at the Green Street Methodist Episcopal Church.

After her sanctification Amanda began attending the Tuesday Meeting for the Promotion of Holiness that was held at the home of Walter and Phoebe Palmer, where she met some of the most important people involved in what was called the Holiness Movement. In keeping with the teachings of the movement, Amanda started dressing plainly, and she and her husband had increasing arguments about changes Amanda wanted to make to achieve a more holy way of living. Their marriage, already in such trouble that James had stopped paying Amanda's rent, suffered a tremendous blow when their only child together became ill with bronchitis, suffered convulsions, and died in Amanda's arms on June 25, 1869. James sent word that he was sick and he did not help pay for the burial or attend the funeral services, which greatly angered Amanda. Five months later, James died of stomach cancer.

With her husband and young children all deceased, Amanda devoted her energies to the Holiness Movement, and she and Mazie started traveling to camp meetings in July 1870. The meetings usually lasted about ten days, and nationally known religious speakers drew huge crowds that numbered in the thousands. The first one Amanda went to was on eighty acres of land near Oakington, Maryland; eight thousand people attended. Camp meetings had become so popular that permanent summer resorts, such as Coney Island, New York, and Atlantic City, New Jersey, were growing up around them. Camp meetings were attended predominantly by whites, but African Americans were welcome and invited to take part in all services. During what were called testimony services, anyone was welcome to speak, and Amanda impressed many in the crowd when she spoke about her religious experiences.

In October 1870 the pastor of the African Methodist Church in Salem, New Jersey, asked Amanda to conduct a revival. Afraid but excited, Amanda made her way to Salem. Her sermon ignited the crowd, which swelled, and the revival meetings lasted for two weeks. After her initial success, Amanda continued to travel and preach at area AME churches through May 1871. At some point she decided to become a full-time evangelist, and she spent her time traveling and preaching. Amanda was a gifted speaker with a wonderful singing voice, and she became a feature at camp meetings. She developed a friendship with John Inskip and his wife, who were both influential in the Holiness Movement, and her preaching began to attract huge crowds. So many crowded around to hear her speak at a camp meeting at Ocean Grove, New Jersey, in August 1874 that other services planned for the afternoon had to be delayed.

Amanda made her living from sporadic donations that were given to her after her sermons at camp meetings. By early 1876 members of the local Methodist church had raised money to buy a house for her, and she moved back to Philadelphia. Unfortunately the money raised covered only two-thirds of the cost of the house, and Amanda was not sure how she was going to raise the additional money she needed. That summer she traveled to Ocean Grove, New Jersey, for the annual Holiness meeting, where she was given free accommodations by the organizers. The public got the impression that Amanda owned two houses; her donations dwindled, and she was plagued by money problems. But as her personal resources went down, her stature in the Holiness Movement increased, and Amanda met many influential leaders of the times. One of those she became friends with was Mary Coffin Johnson, founder of the Woman's Christian Temperance Union (WCTU), of which Amanda was a member. Mary would play a key role in Amanda's life—she would be the one to first invite Amanda to spread her message of Holiness around the world.

In 1878 Mary Coffin Johnson paid Amanda's fare to England on the steamship *Ohio,* and she and Amanda attended the Keswick Conventions together. From there they traveled throughout England attending temperance and Holiness meetings. Johnson returned to the States in February 1879, but Amanda continued to travel overseas. She and another missionary traveled throughout Europe en route to India, where Amanda began preaching by January 1880.

Amanda remained in India until June 1881, when she traveled back to Liverpool, England.

By January 1882 she was working in West Africa as a missionary in Liberia, which had been founded by African Americans from the United States in the 1820s. Her work was supported by sporadic donations and a yearly contribution of about $20 from an Irish woman, very meager income even by missionary standards. Within three weeks of her arrival, she contacted malaria. Although she survived, she would have relapses over the next six years. Amanda spent her time in Liberia traveling and preaching Christianity and temperance, although her efforts met with only limited success. Amanda would not return to England until 1889.

Amanda arrived back in the United States in the fall of 1890 and continued her preaching against temperance and for Christianity. She traveled throughout the country relaying her experiences in Liberia and her feelings against the consumption of alcohol. She felt her main objective, to bring Christianity to others, was often negatively influenced because alcohol kept many from accepting God into their lives. In January 1891 Amanda was part of a delegation that testified before a congressional committee that was considering banning the sale of alcohol to Africa. By the fall of 1892 Amanda had moved to Chicago and decided to write *An Autobiography: The Story of the Lord's Dealings with Mrs. Amanda Smith the Colored Evangelist,* which was published in 1893.

Once done with her book, Amanda began traveling and preaching temperance again. Over time she decided she wanted to open an orphanage and industrial home in the Chicago area for African-American children and began raising funds for her cause in 1895. It took Amanda four years of fund-raising, but the Amanda Smith Orphanage and Industrial Home for Abandoned and Destitute Colored Children officially opened on June 28, 1899. Amanda ran the home herself and paid the operating costs through fund-raising, donations she received at meetings she spoke at, and the profits from her autobiography. Unfortunately the home was constantly struggling financially, and by 1912 Amanda had resigned her position and retired to Sebring, Florida. There she suffered a stroke that left her paralyzed on her left side. She died from a cerebral thrombosis on February 25, 1915. The orphanage and school she established closed its doors in November 1918 when a fire destroyed much of the buildings and killed two girls.

Amanda Berry Smith, although born a slave, spent her life traveling the world spreading Christianity. She never became rich by doing so, but she felt she had a calling that she had to answer. Answering that call would lead her to speak in front of white audiences at a time when race relations were volatile and most African Americans stayed with their own race. Although she sometimes was subjected to degradation because of her race, she always put her own feelings aside in order to fulfill what she felt to be her destiny.

IDA TARBELL

1857-1944

Muckraking Journalist

IDA WAS AMAZED. JUST A SHORT WHILE AGO she had only $150 left to her name, and now she held a check for $100 from *Scribner's* magazine in her hands. Even better than the financial security the money provided was the sense of confidence it fueled. Ida's success so far confirmed that her choice to leave a steady job in Meadville, Pennsylvania, to move to Paris, France, had been a good one. She had written and submitted articles about everyday life in Paris within a week of her arrival in the city, and three newspapers—the *Pittsburgh Dispatch,* the *Cincinnati Times-Star,* and the *Chicago Tribune*—had bought her stories and were interested in buying more on a regular basis. And now Scribner's, the most prestigious magazine in the United States, was publishing a short story she had written.

Although Ida enjoyed a bit of fame when her short story appeared in *Scribner's,* she kept her writing focus on what she did best: articles about everyday life around her. Writing and selling these articles allowed her to stay in Paris and work on the project that had prompted her to travel there in the first place: to write a biography of Madame Roland, a leader of the French Revolution.

IDA TARBELL

Ida had discovered Madame Roland when she began studying the role of female political leaders throughout history to see if their behavior was different from that of men. In the world of the late 1800s that Ida lived in, suffragists were making the case that women receiving the right to vote would make for a better world. Ida was skeptical, and the research she did convinced her women political leaders were no better at caring for the world than their male counterparts. Madame Roland's story, which ended at the guillotine, intrigued Ida, and she dreamed of writing her entire biography one day. Ida's research also resulted in her decision not to support the women's movement in their efforts to win women the right to vote—a lifelong decision that would seem at odds with the reality of her life. Ida, then thirty-three years old, was well educated, had declared her intent never to marry, and supported herself by working as a journalist. But this decision would reveal an integral part of Ida's makeup: She would objectively investigate and make her decisions based on what she found to be true, not on what would be the popular response.

This inherent objectivity that Ida possessed was responsible for her leaving her position as editor of the *Chautauquan,* a magazine she had worked at for six years. Her salary was excellent, but Ida no longer felt challenged. She realized she had to decide between staying at a job that made her feel secure or moving on to Paris and the unknown. By looking at her life so far, Ida concluded that no one was ever really secure—life could pull the rug out from under you at any time—and she decided to take the plunge. Ida had grown up among the boom-and-bust era of the oil industry in Pennsylvania. She had seen neighbors and friends go from rich to penniless, and she knew well how quickly life could take a turn.

Ida was born on November 5, 1857, on her grandparents' farm in Erie County, Pennsylvania. Ida's mother, Esther, was staying with her parents while Ida's father, Frank, built a house for his family in

Iowa, where he planned to be a farmer. Plans for relocating changed with the onset of the Panic of 1857 and the resulting depression that enveloped the country. Frank had to work his way back home, and Ida was a year old by the time he returned to Pennsylvania. Once home, his life of travel continued as he worked as a riverboat captain on the Allegheny and Ohio Rivers.

While journeying home after a trip to Kentucky, Frank Tarbell heard the news that an oil well had been drilled near Titusville, Pennsylvania, and he decided to stop and check out the area. When he saw the number of wells being drilled and heard some well owners boasting they were drilling a hundred barrels of oil a day, Frank decided to use his carpentry skills to make containers that would hold the oil. The wooden containers he made were a success, and in 1860 Frank Tarbell moved his family, which now included Ida's baby brother, William, to a small house he built along Cherry Run Creek outside Titusville.

Ida went from living on a bucolic farm to living in the flatlands of a valley where the grass and trees were coated with black oil. A large oil derrick was right outside their home's front door, and the smell of oil pits punctuated the air. Not long after they arrived, Ida, who was going on three years old, decided she was returning to her grandparents' farm. With her mother's permission, she set out on foot, not stopping until she reached an embankment a few hundred yards from the house. Although the slope wasn't that steep, it seemed like a mountain to Ida. After a good deal of thought, Ida concluded that even if she did find a way up the embankment, she wasn't sure how to get to her grandparents' farm, so the only solution was to return home. Esther found her logic-driven daughter sitting on the front stoop.

Ida soon grew accustomed to her new home. She loved listening to her father's stories of when he was a riverboat captain, and she spent hours studying the nuances of the creek beside their house and the creatures it harbored. The oil business boomed, and Ida's parents were able to buy a home on the hillside above the valley, where the dirt and grime of the oil drilling below could easily be ignored. Ida's family grew to include another sister and brother, and their everyday life was a happy one that was marred by two deaths: President Lincoln and Ida's younger brother of scarlet fever a few years later.

As the oil business evolved, metal containers began to replace wooden ones, and Frank Tarbell began producing oil instead of building oil containers. The area the family lived in eventually grew into a town that was named Rouseville, and the Tarbells were soon living a good life that included an appreciation for music and the arts. Their home grew to include a library, where Ida would voraciously read the publications her father subscribed to, including the *New York Tribune* and *Harper's Weekly* and *Harper's Monthly* magazines.

Just as Ida was settling into a decade of happy existence in Rouseville, her parents announced that the family was moving to Titusville, a bigger town that her parents assured would offer all of them more opportunities. Although initially skeptical of the move, Ida soon adjusted to her new hometown, and the home her father built for the family in Titusville served as an example to Ida of how living your life to obtain security could prove a foolish endeavor. The family's new home was a former hotel that had been built in the town of Pithole for $60,000; after the town's oil boom went bust, Frank Tarbell bought the hotel for $6,000. He had it unassembled, carted the ten miles to Titusville, and rebuilt.

Ida loved her home, especially the tower room, but the impressionable teenager never forgot how easily Pithole had gone from a town of twenty thousand souls to a ghost town within five years.

The family's wealth increased as the oil business in Titusville expanded. Soon railroad tracks passed through the town, and Ida's father and other oil producers used the railroads to ship their crude oil away to be refined. But in February 1872 the railroad announced that it had made an agreement with a group of oil refiners in Cleveland who had formed the South Improvement Company to charge oil refiners not in the company a higher rate to ship their crude oil. By conspiring with the railroad, the South Improvement Company hoped the higher rates would cause the independent refiners to fail. Once the independents were gone, the oil refiners who had formed South Improvement Company would have a monopoly and could sell crude oil at whatever price they chose to set.

Oilmen in the region around Titusville were outraged by the duplicity of their fellow oilmen, and thousands of them formed the Petroleum Producers' Union, which launched a fierce campaign against the South Improvement Company's tactics. When they discovered the mastermind behind the South Improvement Company was John D. Rockefeller, head of Standard Oil Company, the men of the union, including Frank Tarbell, pledged never to ship their oil to his company to be refined. The union eventually prevailed. The railroads backed out of their agreement with the South Improvement Company and returned to charging all refiners the same rates to ship oil.

Ida, who was now in high school, was deeply affected not only by the toll she saw the controversy take on her father but also by the realization that some men were becoming very rich in the new industrial age by utilizing unfair business methods.

She followed the standoff between the union and the South Improvement Company closely, but her main focus during her time at Titusville High School was her discovery of the world of science. Books she found at the high school library showed her that the things she had been collecting for years, such as her pressed leaves and butterflies preserved under glass, were studied in courses called botany and zoology. Ida soon bought her first microscope—and she decided that she would never marry. Instead she would attend

Allegheny College, thirty miles from home in the town of Meadville, and become a scientist. The college, where General Washington had stopped briefly during the Revolutionary War, had begun admitting women in 1870, but Ida was the lone woman among her forty classmates when she enrolled in 1876. When she graduated in 1880, she was immediately offered a job as headmistress at the Poland Union Seminary in Poland, Ohio, and readily accepted. Unfortunately her first job turned out to be a nightmare of outlandish expectations and low pay. She left when her two-year contract was up and returned to her family home in Titusville.

Ida's first foray into the working world had been a disaster, but she was determined to support herself. When Dr. Theodore Flood, a retired Methodist minister, stayed with the Tarbells while speaking at a prayer meeting being held in Titusville, he suggested that Ida join the staff of the *Chautauquan* magazine, where he was the editor. The *Chautauquan,* published in Meadville, had come about as a way for readers who belonged to the Chautauqua Literary and Scientific Circle—a four-year home-reading education course—to keep in touch with one another. The magazine published some of the required readings of the course, and, because readers from across the nation wrote in with questions about what they'd read, someone was needed to annotate the works the magazine published. Ida's job would be to anticipate reader's questions and include answers to the probable questions with the work being published in the magazine.

Ida accepted the part-time position at the *Chautauquan,* moved to Meadville, and began taking graduate classes in science at Allegheny College. She earned her degree in 1883, but rather than pursue a scientific position, Ida stayed on at the *Chautauquan,* learning every aspect of the magazine business and becoming managing editor. What had started out as a part-time lark turned into a six-year career that Ida enjoyed immensely. In addition to her editorial duties, she also wrote some articles for the magazine that covered women's achievements and social issues of the day, such as slums, labor unions, and workers' rights.

During her research on suffragist issues, Ida had discovered Madame Roland, and the idea of living and working in Paris had begun to take hold. After much soul searching, Ida moved to Paris in 1890 with three other girls who planned to stay through the summer only. Ida's plans were open-ended—she would stay in Paris until her biography on Madame Roland was complete. After receiving the $100 check from *Scribner's,* Ida was sure she could support herself as a freelance writer in Paris. She financed the next few years she spent researching the life of Madame Roland by writing articles that were published in newspapers and magazines back in the States.

Some of her articles were distributed to newspapers throughout the country by an agreement she made with a newspaper syndicate created by Samuel S. McClure. Ida met McClure when he dropped by her flat one afternoon and proceeded to tell Ida his entire life history and his plans for starting a new magazine that he said would be different from the country's leading magazines of the time—*Harper's, Atlantic Monthly, Scribner's,* and the *Century.* This new magazine would sell for 10 cents less than the others, and it would appeal to all readers, not just the well-off. Ida thought the magazine was a splendid idea, and she wrote articles for *McClure's Magazine* regularly once it launched in 1893.

Having completed her manuscript on Madame Roland, Ida returned to Titusville in 1893 to do final editing on the project while visiting her family. She had accepted McClure's offer to join the staff of *McClure's Magazine,* and she received her first assignment via an urgent letter from McClure directing her to come to his New York office at once. He needed her to write a biography of Napoleon Bonaparte, and he needed it in less than two months. It was August 1894, and McClure had already announced that a collection of pictures and a biography of Napoleon would be featured in *McClure's Magazine's* November issue. Unfortunately, the owner of the collection, Gardiner Green Hubbard, who had final approval on the story that would accompany his pictures, had rejected the submitted biography, and McClure needed Ida to save the day by writing another biography.

Ida lamented that it had taken her two years to write a biography of Madame Roland, who was certainly a less important figure than Napoleon, but she took the assignment and, by working long hours six days a week, completed it in just six weeks. Hubbard approved her work, and the first installment of the series ran in the November 1894 issue of *McClure's Magazine*. The biography on Napoleon would appear in installments in the magazine through April 1895, and it would earn Ida accolades from Napoleonic scholars. Ida's words also caught the attention of everyday readers, and the fledging magazine's circulation rose from 35,000 to 65,000 copies during the time the series appeared, ensuring its continued existence. Once the serialization was over, Ida's biography on Napoleon was published as a book titled *A Short Life of Napoleon Bonaparte.*

Although Ida had intended to return to Paris after the Napoleon biography was finished, she found she liked the staff at the magazine, especially Sam McClure and his coeditor, John S. Phillips, and she decided to remain in the States. She found continued success with her next assignment for the magazine, a biography covering the early years of Abraham Lincoln. When the first installment of the biography appeared in November 1895, the magazine had a circulation of 190,000 copies. That circulation swelled to 250,000 copies by the time the second installment was issued. *McClure's Magazine* was now the number-one magazine in the nation, and Ida Tarbell was the most well-known woman writer of the time. But Ida had yet to write the story that would bring her everlasting fame—the *History of the Standard Oil Company.*

The success of *McClure's Magazine* was largely attributed to the knack Sam McClure had for knowing what subjects the public wanted to read about. At first the magazine had featured stories about famous people, but by 1900 McClure felt the nation was interested in reading about social issues of the day. He decided that trusts formed by companies to monopolize their industries by driving competitors out of business would make a good subject for a series, and he assigned Ida to write it. It was decided that the best way to explain the actions of trusts was to pick one industry to concentrate on and show through that industry's history how the trust came about and how it impacted its industry and the lives of the people who worked in the industry.

The Standard Oil Company was the first trust that had formed in the United States, and it dominated the oil industry. The trust had originally begun as the South Improvement Company, and Ida remembered well the battle her father and the other men around Titusville had fought to defeat the unfair practices the railroads and the trust tried to inflict on independent oil refiners when Ida was just a teenager. When Ida took on this first assignment in her series on trusts, she hoped to prove that unethical business practices by some capitalists—not capitalism in its own right—was what led to corruption in business.

Ida immersed herself in her research, poring over court documents and other public records involving the trust. Her endeavor was greatly helped when Mark Twain introduced her to Henry Rogers, a vice president at Standard Oil. At their first meeting, Ida and Henry realized they had both grown up near the same area in the oil region of Pennsylvania, although Henry was about twenty years older than Ida. Henry agreed to give Ida information on the Standard Oil Company, reasoning that his cooperation would help Ida see the trust in a favorable light. The two met on a regular, though clandestine, basis. Ida agreed to discuss anything she discovered with Rogers so he could explain the company's position, but she made it clear that she would tell the story as she saw it.

The first installment of the *History of the Standard Oil Company* was printed in *McClure's Magazine* in November 1902. It was a complete article in itself, a method employed by the magazine with all its series. That way, a series could be ended easily if public interest in the subject subsided. But interest for Ida's series would not wane; it ran for almost two years, with the last of nineteen installments appearing in the October 1904 issue, and the entire series was immediately reprinted in book form.

One of the most dramatic installments carried proof that accusations by independent oil producers that Standard Oil Company was interfering with their shipments of oil were true. Ida obtained the actual documents proving the company's sabotage of one man's business when an office boy at Standard Oil happened to glance at the papers he was burning as part of his normal work routine and noticed the name of someone he knew—an independent oil refiner. The office boy salvaged documents showing how the trust ensured that the man's oil shipments were not delivered.

The office boy gave the documents to the oilman, and the oilman gave them to Ida. Keeping to the agreement she had made with Harry Rogers, Ida asked Rogers for an explanation, but he denied that the company was involved in such practices. When Ida next visited Rogers at his office, the most recent issue of *MClure's Magazine* was opened to her article detailing the information she had been given. When asked, Ida wouldn't reveal the source of the documents that were the basis for the article, and that was the last time she and Harry met.

Ida's series on the Standard Oil Company ushered in a new type of journalism that would become known as muckraking. Ida and other muckrakers, such as Upton Sinclair and fellow *McClure's Magazine* writers Lincoln Steffens and Frank Norris, swept up the "dirt" by exposing corruption in business and politics and social wrongs that were happening in the early twentieth century. Their methods set them apart because they approached their subjects as if they were historians and they applied journalistic standards to their investigations. Muckrakers were known for providing detailed documentation supporting their conclusions, and Ida's *History of the Standard Oil Company* was heralded as the best example of the methods of investigative journalism employed by the muckrakers. Ida's work exposed unfair business practices used by trusts, and it greatly contributed to the social and political atmosphere in which the U.S. Supreme Court ruled in 1911 to dissolve the Standard Oil Trust.

The *History of the Standard Oil Company* made Ida a household name, but her journalistic contributions to society were far from over. After another two years at *McClure's Magazine,* she and fellow magazine staffers left to start their own enterprise, the *American Magazine.* Ida contributed many investigative stories to its pages before it folded in 1914 due to spiraling publishing costs, and she also continued to publish books on Abraham Lincoln. In her late fifties by then, Ida had no intention of retiring. She joined a lecture circuit and gave forty-nine lectures within the same number of days in forty-nine different towns. Her second lecture tour had begun when she received a telegram in 1917 from President Woodrow Wilson asking her to join the Woman's Committee of the Council of National Defense. Ida canceled her tour and headed to Washington, where she helped organize ways for women to help in the war effort.

After the war, Ida returned to Paris and joined the staff of *Red Cross Magazine,* where she wrote a series of articles on the work the Red Cross was accomplishing in the war-ravaged area. In 1920 Ida once again rejected the constraints of employment security and returned to freelance writing. She continued her study of Lincoln, publishing more books on her favorite subject, and at age eighty-one her autobiography, *All in the Day's Work,* was published.

Ida kept writing until her death in January 1944 of pneumonia. Her body was laid to rest in her hometown of Titusville, Pennsylvania.

A postage stamp with her image on it was issued in September 2002, a testament to the fact that Ida Tarbell's contributions to journalism—and the changes in business practices her writing brought about—are still remembered today.

NELLIE BLY

1864-1922

Undercover Reporter

THE CRIES NELLIE BLY HEARD WERE COMING FROM OUTSIDE, and there was no doubt the woman screaming was insane. A momentary chill pierced Nellie's bravado as she realized she was now a part of this woman's world, but she determined to carry on and find out all she could before someone discovered her ruse. She struck up a conversation with one of the three other women in the room with her, and Nellie realized quite quickly that the woman was as sane as she was. The next woman Nellie talked to definitely was not sane, though, and the third woman said her case was hopeless and then refused to talk anymore. After her conversations, Nellie began to feel more confident of her ability to deceive those around her, and she felt sure she would achieve her ultimate goal—to spend ten days as an inmate at the Woman's Lunatic Asylum on Blackwell Island, 120 acres of land located in New York's East River.

The year was 1887, and Nellie was on assignment for the *New York World* newspaper. The paper's managing editor, Col. John Cockerill, had promised her a job if she could get this story, and although she doubted he believed she would actually succeed, Nellie was

NELLIE BLY

determined to land the position. Pink, as Nellie was known to her family and friends back in Pittsburgh, Pennsylvania, was not the type of girl who gave up easily.

The twenty-three-year-old had already overcome many obstacles since her birth as Elizabeth Jane Cochran on May 5, 1864, at Cochran's Mills in western Pennsylvania. Her father was a prominent businessman and elected official known to everyone in the area as the Judge, and her mother was the Judge's second wife. Mary Jane Cummings, a widow, had married the Judge in 1858 after his first wife, with whom he had ten children, had died in 1857. Mary Jane and the Judge had two boys before Elizabeth Jane came along. Mary Jane dressed her daughter in pink rather than the drab gray, brown, and black colors that most mothers in the area chose for their daughters, which is how Elizabeth Jane got the nickname Pink. The Cochrans would have two more children after Pink—a daughter named Catherine and a son named Harry.

Pink's early childhood was idyllic, but everything changed when her father died unexpectedly when she was six years old. The Judge did not have a will, and his assets, including the mansion the family recently had moved to in the small nearby town of Apollo, were liquidated and distributed among his fifteen children. Pink's mother got a modest widow's share, and her children's shares of the estate were managed by the town banker, Col. Samuel Jackson. Mary Jane's family moved from the mansion into a modest frame house two blocks away. They weren't poor, and Mary Jane still found money for Pink to have piano and horseback-riding lessons, but they were no longer living lavishly.

In 1879 it was decided Pink would go to boarding school at the State Normal School in Indiana, fifteen miles east of Apollo. She was to become a teacher, one of the few occupations open to women at the time. Colonel Jackson assured Pink there was enough money to cover the three years of education required for her to obtain her degree. When Pink enrolled, she signed her name as Elizabeth J.

Cochrane, losing the nickname Pink and adding an *e* to her last name. But after not even one complete term, Colonel Jackson advised Pink that her money was running low, and she eventually dropped out of school due to lack of funds. When Mary Jane followed her two older sons to Pittsburgh and set up a home for them, Pink and her two younger siblings were in tow. Pink, who was then sixteen, spent the next four years trying to find a decent job, not an easy feat for a woman in the 1880s.

Pink enjoyed reading the column titled "Quiet Observations" that was carried in the *Pittsburg Dispatch* newspaper. Written by Erasmus Wilson, the column was signed simply Q. O. Wilson was Pittsburgh's most popular columnist of the time, and he used his down-home observations to look at familiar subjects in new ways. Pink's interest was especially piqued when Q. O. wrote several columns dealing with the current role of women in society, often using the term the "women's sphere" to describe areas women should excel in, such as sewing, cooking, and keeping house. His columns set off a firestorm of reaction across Pittsburgh.

Pink felt compelled to write to Q. O., someone she pictured as old and sour-faced. Her letter rebutted Q. O.'s view of how women should fit into the world with a harsh dose of reality, pointing out that a girl in her position, with no father, had very little chance of advancing herself out of her working-class situation. She signed her letter Little Orphan Girl, since no self-respecting woman of the day would commit social suicide by signing her real name to a letter written to a newspaper. Her letter caught the eye of George Madden, managing editor of the *Dispatch,* who was impressed with the earnest way Little Orphan Girl presented her argument. He thought the writer of the letter had potential as a newspaper reporter, and a note was placed in the paper's Letters to the Editor section asking the writer known as Little Orphan Girl to send her name and address to the office.

Pink saw the note, but she wasn't about to just send her name and address—she traveled to the office the day after the note appeared on January 17, 1885. After rushing up four flights of stairs, she met George Madden, not the big man with a beard and spectacles she had imagined but a pleasant boy, and Q. O., also not the sourpuss she had imagined but instead a good-natured guy. Madden didn't print her letter, but he did ask her to write another article on women in society, which he paid her for.

Pink was eventually made part of the *Dispatch* staff, and Madden realized she would need a byline, since women who wrote for newspapers never used their real names. Madden asked the others in the newsroom for suggestions, and among the names thrown out for consideration was Nelly Bly, made famous by a song written by Pittsburgh's Stephen Collins Foster thirty-five years earlier. Madden, pressured by deadlines, quickly decided on Nellie Bly, misspelling the name.

Nellie's first series consisted of eight articles that detailed her visits to factories throughout the city. Her attention to detail made the lives of the poor women working in factories real and touching, and the series garnered attention. But after the series, Nellie was assigned to cover items traditionally considered women's interest, such as fashion and society news. She soon grew bored and decided she would journey to Mexico and send travelogues back to the newspaper, a daring plan for a young woman at that time. Nellie and her mother traveled in Mexico for almost six months. When they returned home and Nellie returned to her position at the *Dispatch,* she soon found herself again covering what she considered to be boring assignments on women's issues. Eventually she just stopped going to work, and one day Erasmus Wilson found a note from Nellie that simply stated: "Dear Q. O. – I am off for New York. Look out for me."

Nellie's search for a job in New York did not progress as quickly as she had envisioned when she wrote her note. She arrived in May 1887, and the meeting where she presented her ideas to Colonel Cockerill of the *New York World* didn't happen until September. By that time Nellie was just about out of money, and she was thrilled when the colonel gave her $25 to keep her from going to rival newspapers with her ideas before he had a chance to decide whether he wanted to hire her. At their next meeting, Colonel Cockerill offered her a full-time position with the paper if she could get committed to an insane asylum. Asylums were being covered heavily in the news, and there were many questions being raised about their conditions and how patients were treated.

Nellie, ecstatic at the thought of a permanent position at the paper, readily agreed to get herself committed. Colonel Cockerill and she decided that Nellie would take the name Nellie Brown, so her initials would remain intact, and she would remain in the asylum for ten days, when the paper would have her released. How she was to get herself committed had been left up to Nellie, so she practiced looking crazy in her mirror at home and then rented a room at a working-class boardinghouse. There she pretended she was afraid of the other renters because she thought they were insane, and she sat up all night and refused to sleep. The other women eventually decided that Nellie was the insane one, and the police were summoned. The police brought Nellie before a judge, who called in a doctor to determine if Nellie was sane. Nellie had fooled the judge and the doctor, and she was now a patient at the insane ward of Bellevue Hospital, the last step before being shipped to Blackwell Island.

She was dozing in a chair when a man sat down beside her, took her pulse, inspected her tongue, and began asking her questions, most of which Nellie would later recall in her book *Ten Days in a Mad-House* as being "useless and senseless." After a few minutes, the man, who by now Nellie realized was a doctor, turned to the nurse and declared Nellie "positively demented." With that diagnosis, Nellie was left alone again for the duration of the day. A second doctor visited Nellie in her room during the night, and he assured her that she was quite sick, even though she told him she felt all right in response to his inquiry. The rest of the night passed without Nellie getting much sleep, mostly because of the nurses, who, when they weren't walking heavily down the hallways every half hour to check on each patient, were reading aloud and talking to one another about the patients.

The next morning Nellie was taken into a sitting room where yet another doctor asked her a few questions and quickly dismissed her. That afternoon, one of the doctors examined Nellie again, again asking a few irrelevant questions and then having her stretch out her arms and move her fingers, which Nellie did immediately on cue. Nellie then spent another cold night in her room, and the next morning she and the other patients were told they would be leaving Bellevue that afternoon.

Finally Nellie was transported on a filthy boat and committed to the Women's Insane Asylum on Blackwell Island. As the asylum door lock clicked shut, Nellie's heart gave a sharp twinge. She knew she was sane and would be released from this place, but she was about to become a companion of the insane on a twenty-four-hour basis, and the thought was understandably frightening. Nellie was also disconcerted that four doctors so far had seen fit to declare her insane on very little, if any, evidence of the fact.

One by one, the women she had traveled with from Bellevue to the island were brought before another doctor. Nellie listened as one woman rationally explained, to no avail, that she was not insane and as another tried, also to no avail, to explain in German that she did not speak English. When Nellie's turn came, she was determined not to act any differently than she would if she were free, except she wouldn't tell who she was or where her home was. Although she answered the doctor's questions and even made a point of saying she wasn't sick and didn't want to be there, the doctor paid more attention to the nurse than to Nellie. He wrote some notes regarding Nellie and sent her back to wait with the others.

Later that evening, after a practically inedible meal, the group of newcomers was instructed to follow one of the nurses to the bathroom, where other staff members waited. Nellie was told to undress, and as she protested she spied, as she would later recount in her newspaper article and book, "one of the craziest women in the ward standing by the filled bathtub with a large, discolored rag in her hands." Attendants stripped Nellie's clothes off, and Nellie jumped into the tub to avoid being naked in front of everyone.

The water was cold, and Nellie continued protesting against the bath and having an audience. She was told to shut up, and the crazy woman began to scrub her from head to toe. The rinsing process consisted of three buckets of water being poured over Nellie's head in quick succession. Then, as she would later describe it in her newspaper account:

> . . . they dragged me, gasping, shivering and quaking, from the tub. For once I did look insane. I caught a glance of the indescribable look on the faces of my companions, who had witnessed my fate and knew theirs was surely following. Unable to control myself at the absurd picture I presented, I burst into roars of laughter. They put me, dripping wet, into a short canton flannel slip, labeled across the extreme and in large black letters, "Lunatic Asylum, B. I., H. 6." The letters meant Blackwell's Island, Hall 6.

Nellie was locked in a room that contained nothing but her bed. She shivered under a wool blanket too small to cover both her shoulders and her feet at the same time. Throughout the long night, Nellie worried what would happen if there was a fire. All the women's rooms were locked, and the windows had bars on the outside. Considering the treatment she had received from the nurses so far, Nellie doubted they would have the presence of mind, let alone the caring concern, that would be needed to release all the patients from their rooms.

The next morning nurses arrived in Nellie's room at 5:30 a.m. and roughly told her to put on the clothing they flung on the floor. When Nellie asked for her own clothing back, she was told by the head nurse, Miss Grady, that she should take what she got and keep quiet. By now Nellie understood this recurring theme: The patients were charity cases and should therefore be grateful for what they got, no matter how inadequate it might be. With hair still damp from her "bath" the night before, Nellie put the clothes on. The underskirt was six inches longer than the skirt over it.

Next the patients were taken to the bathroom. Here Nellie realized that forty-five women were meant to share two coarse towels. Nellie decided her long underskirt would have to play double duty as a towel. The women were then instructed to sit on a bench that was brought in, and one patient and two nurses used six combs on the heads of all the patients. They were anything but gentle while doing so, and no concern was shown for the possibility of spreading the sores some of the women had on their scalps. Nellie set her teeth and endured the pain of the combing. Her hair was then tied in one plait and secured with a rag, a procedure that was applied to all the patients.

From the bathroom the patients proceeded to a sitting room, where they milled about until they were told to line up and then marched to the dining room, where Nellie again found the food to be inedible. After the meal, the patients returned to the sitting room. The new patients went to see the doctor, while the others were assigned cleaning chores. Later in the afternoon, the women gathered shawls and were led out of the building. As nurses stood guard,

Nellie and about 1,600 other women were marched about on the walkways, but no one was allowed on the beautifully manicured lawns. After the walk, dinnertime arrived; Nellie forced herself to eat, successfully choking down all but the crusts of one slice of bread. The fact that the women had spied wonderful fruits, breads, and meats when their walk had taken them past the kitchen where food was prepared for the nurses and doctors only made the meal harder to swallow. After dinner the women returned to the sitting room, where they had to sit on straight-back benches. If they talked they were told to shut up; if they dared to get up, they were told to sit down and be still.

Nellie's ten days at the asylum would mirror the activities of this first day, and Nellie and the other women had no choice but to endure the bad food, the cold, the lack of adequate clothing and concern for hygiene, and the harsh treatment they received from the nurses. Nellie saw nurses tease patients unmercifully and drag patients away, and she heard the patients screaming as they were being beaten. Once a week the patients were given a bath in a tub filled with water that wasn't changed between patients. The water was dumped only when it became thick, and then the tub was immediately refilled and the bathing continued.

Nellie managed to meet many of the forty-five women who were assigned to her hall, and she realized she was not the only sane inmate being held at the Woman's Lunatic Asylum on Blackwell Island. When she was transferred to Hall 7, she also discovered sane women residing there. There were, of course, many women at the asylum who *were* insane. Nellie got less than her usual minimal amount of sleep one night when she was locked in a room with six other women, one of whom kept leaving her bed and creeping around the room searching for someone to kill. The doctors who saw the patients didn't believe anything the patients said, and the patients eventually stopped reporting things that happened. Nellie told every doctor she saw that she was sane and urged that her sanity be tested, but it was clear that her insanity was a foregone conclusion.

After Nellie had been an inmate for ten days, the newspaper sent a lawyer who arranged for her release. In no time she was a free woman heading back to New York City to put her experiences on paper. She was released on October 4, and the first installment of her exposé appeared in the *World* on October 9. The story, and Nellie, caught the imagination of the public, and Nellie Bly became famous. Many people had written about insane asylums, but only Nellie Bly actually had herself committed in order to get the real story. Her newspaper report was later published as a book titled *Ten Days in a Mad-House,* and a grand jury was convened to investigate the asylum. The changes Nellie had suggested in her report were recommended by the grand jury, and more funds were allotted for the budgets of mental asylums. Nellie's name soon became synonymous with undercover reporting, and she wrote many other exposés on the social issues of the day.

Nellie grabbed headlines again in 1889 when the *World* created a publicity stunt to increase readership by sending her around the world in an effort to beat the time taken by the characters in the book *Around the World in Eighty Days.* Nellie not only completed the 24,899-mile trip in less time, she did it alone, unaccompanied by a male—a first for women at that time. She also defied the common notion that women could not travel lightly; she carried all her belonging in one piece of hand luggage that was no more than sixteen inches wide and seven inches tall.

In 1895 Nellie surprised everyone by marrying Robert Seaman, a millionaire forty-four years her elder. She retired from journalism for the most part, and they remained married until Seaman's death nine years later at age eighty. By this time Nellie had taken over the running of some of his companies, in particular the Iron Clad Manufacturing Company. She was a hard worker, often putting in twelve-hour days, and she could run every machine in the plant. Nellie also designed some new machines and by 1905 held twenty-five patents in her own name.

The health of her workers was paramount to Nellie, and she introduced health care plans and built libraries and gyms for the workers to use. Unfortunately, due to mismanagement by people Nellie trusted, the company went bankrupt. After a long drawn-out court battle over issues with the company, Nellie left to visit friends in Austria for a much-needed rest. That rest would turn into a five-year stay caused by World War I. Nellie delayed her departure for too long and was no longer allowed to leave the country once America entered the war on the side opposing Austria.

When Nellie finally was able to return to the United States, she was in her fifties and looking for a job. She was hired by the New York newspaper *Evening Journal* to write a column about the needs of abandoned children, a cause that she became passionate about. Nellie worked right up to the end of her life. She caught pneumonia while covering a story for the *Journal* and passed away on January 27, 1922.

MARY ENGLE PENNINGTON

1872-1952

Refrigeration Specialist

WHEN MARY ENGLE PENNINGTON INVITED GUESTS TO DINNER, she was showing off her skills as a scientist, not as a chef. Mary served frozen food at her dinners, and she was quite proud to do so. After all, the refrigeration techniques Mary had developed were what allowed companies to store and ship frozen and perishable food to grocery stores without it spoiling.

When frozen foods were introduced to the American public in the 1930s, Mary was already known for her landmark research on the best techniques for getting food from the farmer to the consumer without it being contaminated by bacteria. She owned her own company—a consulting firm to the sector of the food industry involved in handling, storing, and transporting perishable food—that she had opened in 1922 in New York City. All aspects of the burgeoning frozen food industry captivated Mary's interest, and she soon concentrated much of her work on it. She designed and oversaw the building of refrigerated warehouses and also designed and built refrigerator-freezers for commercial and home use.

Mary's contributions meant consumers could trust that the frozen food they bought in the grocery store was safe, and they were able to store at home what they bought without fear of spoilage. She enjoyed great success as a consultant, which enabled her to reside in a penthouse on Riverside Drive in New York City, but monetary gain was not what motivated Mary Engle Pennington. Her life had been dedicated to science since she had opened a library book on medical chemistry at the age of twelve and discovered there was a world composed of atoms and molecules that she couldn't see that was real nonetheless. Although she didn't understand much of what she read, she had found a new world she wanted to explore.

Showing the logical, scientific thought patterns she would display throughout her life, Mary visited the college that was four blocks from her house to get answers to the questions engendered by her poring over the library book. The astonished professors at the University of Pennsylvania told the twelve-year-old before them to come back when she was older, and Mary showed her straightforward nature when she did just that. She would continue to study the invisible world that makes up the world we do see for the rest of her life—a journey that would result in safer handling of food all along its path from farmer to consumer.

The inquisitive child who searched out the answers she needed was still very much a part of the eighty-year-old woman who was entertaining dinner guests. Although she had officially retired from the workforce, she still did some consulting from time to time besides fulfilling her duties as the vice president of the American Institute of Refrigeration.

Like all Americans during the 1940s and 1950s, Mary discovered new foods available at the grocery store every time she visited. Dinner choices at her house could now include hors d'oeuvres before the main course and whipped topping on the ice cream served for dessert. Besides packaged meat and fish, main entrees could now include meat pies, pizza, and Mexican foods. French fries had made their way onto dinner tables everywhere as a new way of serving potatoes that seemed to go with almost any entree. And of course, frozen vegetables and fruits were meal staples.

Not every scientist is fortunate enough to see their research and techniques applied in ways that revolutionize how people live, but Mary Engle Pennington witnessed the application of her scientific successes every time she went to the grocery store. And her impact was not only felt in the frozen food sections; her techniques also allowed the perishable foods now sold to get to the stores without spoilage and to stay that way until they had been consumed. For example, the egg carton that rested at the top of so many shoppers' grocery bags had been invented by Mary to keep eggs from breaking on their way to market.

The innovations Mary saw around her did not tell the whole story of Mary's life, though. As with any successful woman in the 1950s, Mary's road to recognition and acceptance in her field had been long and not easily traveled. Her start in life began in Nashville, Tennessee, on October 8, 1872, where Mary was born to Henry and Sarah Pennington. Shortly afterward, her family moved to Philadelphia to be closer to her mother's relatives, the Engles.

Henry Pennington started a successful label manufacturing business, and he relaxed by gardening while not at work. Mary spent many hours outside with her father in his garden, developing a love of flowers that would last her lifetime. But chemistry, not botany, would be the science that had Mary looking at the world differently from most twelve-year-olds. She thought about molecules and oxygen and how things that were invisible still had a great impact on mankind. The invisible world became very real when she realized that everything on Earth would die without the unseen oxygen around her that no one paid attention to.

Mary's interest in chemistry continued, and after graduating from high school she applied to the University of Pennsylvania, just as the professors she had visited there six years earlier had advised her to. The private school that traced its history from 1740 allowed women to enroll and take classes but conferred bachelor's degrees only on men. Mary earned her certificate of proficiency from the Towne Scientific School of the University of Pennsylvania in 1892, signifying that she had completed all the course work required for a Bachelor of Science degree. Supportive teachers convinced her to remain at the university to take postgraduate classes, and the same school that had denied her a bachelor's degree awarded her a doctorate in chemistry in 1895, when Mary was only twenty-two. Mary then spent an additional two years at the university conducting research in chemical botany and another year of research in physiological chemistry at Yale University in Connecticut. She returned to Philadelphia and opened the Philadelphia Clinical Laboratory after visiting local doctors and getting their assurances that they would use her services. There she applied her knowledge as a bacteriologist by doing analyses for the doctors, and her excellent work resulted in her being asked to lecture at the Woman's Medical College of Pennsylvania. She joined the faculty of the school in 1898 as a professor of physiological chemistry and director of the clinical laboratory. In 1904 Mary began working at the Philadelphia Bureau of Health as the director of its bacteriological laboratory. Her job was to make sure milk and other dairy products sold in the city were safe, a major health concern at that time.

Mary quickly realized that sweeping reform would have to be implemented along every step of the process that brought food from farmers to Philadelphians. She also realized that the call for such changes would be met by resistance from farmers and food vendors unless the situation was handled very delicately. Being the straightforward person she was, Mary decided to meet personally with farmers and vendors in the city and convince them of the need for better procedures to ensure the safety of the food they produced and sold.

By taking this approach, Mary was able to explain how it was possible to reduce the likelihood of people getting sick from eating contaminated food by following the guidelines on handling, storing, and shipping dairy products that she had developed. Mary took a warm and hands-on approach with dairy farmers. She showed them how unsanitary conditions on their farms would result in bacteria growing in their dairy products, and these bacteria would make people sick when they drank the farmers' milk or ate their dairy products. Her logical explanations had the desired effect, and farmers began implementing procedures to ensure sanitary conditions, including inspecting the milk they produced before shipping it.

To convince ice-cream vendors that their food might be making people sick, Mary showed them slides full of bacteria that had been found growing in their ice-cream buckets. Then she showed them how the bacteria could be killed by boiling their buckets. By the time Mary publicly called for laws on the safe production and handling of dairy foods, she had the backing of Philadelphia's farmers and vendors. Some of her innovations were adopted nationwide, such as the standards she developed for preserving milk.

Mary's success in reducing the occurrences of food poisoning by teaching about the unseen bacteria that could make people sick got her noticed by Harvey Wiley, chief chemist in the United States Department of Agriculture (USDA) since 1882. Wiley was also a public health crusader whose lobbying greatly contributed to the passing of the 1906 Pure Food and Drug Act. This act created the Food and Drug Administration (FDA), which was charged with making sure food and medicines sold in the United States were safe.

Harvey Wiley encouraged Mary to take the Civil Service exam so she could work for the USDA. To be sure her gender didn't keep her from being hired, Wiley advised her to sign her name on the application as M. E. Pennington. The ruse worked. Mary was hired by the USDA as a bacteriologist chemist, and she continued to use her initials on the documentation she generated. In 1908 Wiley promoted her to chief of a new research lab that was also created as a result of the 1906 Pure Food and Drug Act. The Food Research Laboratory was located in Philadelphia at Mary's insistence, and she and four employees conducted the scientific research necessary for the government to prosecute cases involving unsafe food handling.

Mary often served as an expert witness on food safety in cases the FDA was prosecuting, but there were still numerous shocked attendees when Mary stood up and addressed the First International Congress of Refrigeration in 1908. This was the first time many in the all-male audience learned that M. E. Pennington was a woman.

M. E. Pennington was now a government administrator, but she continued to spend many hours working alongside her staff in the laboratory. Under her direction, the laboratory would grow to employ forty-five scientists, and its mission would evolve into researching the safe handling and storing of food, especially poultry, eggs, and fish.

Just as she had when she began working for the city of Philadelphia, Mary visited farms to observe operations and discuss the techniques used directly with the farmers. Once again, Mary's warm, straightforward approach was successful. She convinced farmers to collect eggs faster in warm weather because of the increased possibility of bacteria growing in the heat, and she developed an egg carton to protect the eggs during shipping from the farm to the market. After visiting several poultry farms, Mary invented a sharp-pointed knife that made handling and plucking chickens after their slaughter easier, which resulted in more sanitary conditions after the widespread adoption of its use. Mary's firsthand knowledge of the poultry industry allowed her to meticulously identify and implement better procedures along each step of getting a chicken from the farm to the consumer's plate.

Much of Mary's research centered on finding the best temperature to refrigerate foods in order to inhibit the growth of bacteria, since bacteria makes foods spoil. The need for food refrigeration became more and more important as Americans began migrating from the country to cities in the early 1900s. Farmers who used to take their goods to the local market could now reach more buyers in the cities, and products could be shipped greater distances by the trains that now crossed much of America. However, the greater distances food traveled increased the likelihood it would be spoiled by its arrival. Refrigerated boxcars were supposed to keep food cold while in transport, but the research Mary conducted for the government during World War I exposed how woefully inadequate most refrigerated cars were.

As a known refrigeration expert, Mary was asked to consult with the War Shipping Administration to determine the state of the forty thousand refrigerated train cars the government owned and planned to ship food in during the war. Mary found only three thousand were truly fit for use, and she went to work researching and determining the best techniques to be applied to food transportation by rail. She recommended new standards for refrigerated cars and, most important, solved the humidity-control issues inherent in cold storage. Before her work, food would often dry out from the drop in humidity that occurred at low temperatures, or food would spoil from the humidity being too high. Once again, Mary decided hands-on research was necessary and logged many miles riding trains and testing the adequacy of the refrigerated cars.

Mary was awarded the Notable Service Medal for her efforts during the war, and the standards she established in 1917 still served as the blueprint for building refrigerated boxcars twenty-five years later.

MARY ENGLE PENNINGTON ON A BOXCAR

She left government service in 1919 to take a position leading the research and development department of the American Balsa Company, which manufactured insulating materials. The new position meant leaving Philadelphia for New York, which would become her new home. Three years later Mary decided to draw on her knowledge of handling, storing, and transporting perishable foods to open her own consulting firm. Her reputation in the field made her a sought-after commodity, and she traveled extensively across the United States meeting with clients, logging up to fifty thousand miles on the road a year.

But the everyday tasks of running a successful business didn't keep Mary out of the laboratory. Her scientific mind was intrigued by all the advances taking place in the perishable food industry, especially in the new sector of frozen foods. Mary researched which fruits and vegetables were best suited for freezing and the best ways to freeze them. She designed refrigerated warehouses to store products before they were shipped and refrigerated coolers and commercial freezers for displaying products in grocery stores. Following the logical path that food follows from producer to consumer, Mary also designed refrigerators for household use so that consumers could maintain the safety of the food they bought after they brought it home.

Mary's lifelong efforts to improve the safety of food included writing pamphlets for consumers on the safe handling of food in the kitchen and coauthoring a book titled *Eggs*. She also earned several honors. The American Society of Heating, Refrigeration and Air-conditioning Engineers (ASHRAE) named her the foremost American authority on home refrigeration in 1923, and in 1940 the American Chemical Society awarded her the Garvan Medal to recognize her contributions to chemistry. Mary also enjoyed many "firsts" while pursuing the secrets of the unseen world around her: In 1947 she was the first woman admitted to the American Society of Refrigerating Engineers, and in 1959 she was the first woman elected to the Poultry Historical Society's Hall of Fame.

Mary Engle Pennington died on December 27, 1952, but the contributions she made to modern living are apparent in every grocery store across America. Before her innovative designs and techniques were implemented, spoiled food caused thousands of deaths. Her research not only saved lives, it allowed the introduction of many more options in America's food choices.

FLORENCE SEIBERT

1897–1991

Disease Fighter

FLORENCE SEIBERT MADE SOME NOTES, cleaned up, and got ready to head home. Her latest experiment hadn't been successful, but she had learned from it, so it was by no means a failure. She would have to start over, applying what she had learned didn't work to what she knew did. After all the years Florence had spent in a laboratory, she knew scientific breakthroughs resulted from careful observations, copious notes, detailed analysis, and lots of trial and error.

So far Florence had spent almost a decade developing a more reliable skin test for tuberculosis, a highly contagious disease that attacked the lungs. An infected person would develop a cough and sometimes a low-grade fever. The symptoms would progress to spitting up sputum, loss of appetite and resulting weight loss, and trouble breathing. By this time, the sick person often had a wasted look, and death was likely. The disease was transmitted by droplets of fluid released into the air when an infected person coughed, sneezed, or even just exhaled, so any proximity to a sick person could result in another person getting infected. People with tuberculosis were isolated in sanitariums; there was no cure, and the only treatment was rest and a nutritious diet.

Tuberculosis was often referred to as the White Plague because of the number of lives it claimed. German scientist Heinrich Koch identified tubercle bacilli as the bacterium that caused tuberculosis in 1882, when the disease was responsible for one of every seven deaths in Europe. Eight years later he developed a skin test for the disease, and his breakthrough work earned him the 1905 Nobel Prize for medicine. But there was a problem with his test—it didn't always give the right results. Koch's test injected what he called tuberculin, which he made by growing tubercle bacilli in beef broth, under the skin. If the area turned hard, swollen, and red within a few days, it meant the bacterium that caused tuberculosis was present in the person's body.

Unfortunately, Koch wasn't able to isolate the active substance in tuberculin that was responsible for the skin reaction. Scientists came to call this elusive substance pure tuberculin. Because tuberculin couldn't be separated from the impurities that were attached to it, it was never clear how much pure tuberculin actually was injected under the skin. If the injection had less pure tuberculin and more impurities, a person with active tuberculosis might not react to the skin test. Often by the time tuberculosis was correctly diagnosed, the disease was so far advanced that the person would die. People who came in contact with the misdiagnosed patient were also infected.

If Florence was able to separate pure tuberculin from its impurities, the skin test could always have only pure tuberculin in it. That would make test results more accurate, and deaths from misdiagnosed tuberculosis less likely. So when an experiment reached its conclusion without the separation she was looking for happening, Florence began again, applying what she had discovered to her next attempt. Her colleague, Dr. Long, had created a synthetic broth to grow tubercle bacilli in that produced a consistent tuberculin, which had been a giant breakthrough. Now that the tubercle bacilli were no longer grown in beef broth, tuberculin no longer had protein impurities attached to it. Florence's challenge was to separate the pure tuberculin from the remaining impurities.

When the tests Florence performed on tuberculin proved that the substance was a protein, as had long been suspected, she knew the task of making pure tuberculin was going to be formidable. Purifying a protein was considered one of the toughest jobs a scientist could take on. But Florence never had to look far for inspiration to continue her research.

The Philadelphia neighborhood around the Phipps Institute where she worked was full of people who desperately needed her to succeed. For some, their very lives depended on it. The clinic and lab where she worked at Seventh and Lombard Streets had purposefully been located in a congested, poor neighborhood where overcrowding sometimes led to people living in unclean circumstances—the perfect conditions for tuberculosis to develop. The location allowed infected people to walk to the clinic for help. It also provided scientists working in the institute's lab a real-time and evolving research group.

After a decade of research, Florence finally was successful in isolating pure tuberculin in the mid-1930s. She developed a purification process that used filters made from porous clay and cotton that had been treated with nitric acid to produce the desired results. The pure tuberculin was named PPD, which stood for purified protein derivative. Florence helped to produce large quantities of her PPD commercially, which were made available for tuberculosis testing and medical research. Because of her groundbreaking work in isolating PPD and the advances it brought about in the accuracy of the skin test for tuberculosis, Florence was awarded the National Tuberculosis Association's Trudeau Gold Medal in 1938.

Florence had achieved her goal of isolating pure tuberculin, but she knew her fight against tuberculosis was far from over. Her next goal was to determine a standard dosage to be used in the skin test. With a standard dose, doctors didn't need to worry that a reaction was caused by skin sensitivity or different PPD substances used in the injection. It took Florence until 1941 to develop PPD-S, purified protein derivative-standard, and batches of it were set aside to serve as the national standard. In 1942 PPD-S was adopted by the World Health Organization as the standard skin test for tuberculosis around the world. Untold numbers of people were saved from the horrible consequences of tuberculosis because Florence's work made the skin test an accurate indicator of the presence of tubercle bacilli in the body.

It was fitting that the scientific research Florence accomplished was used for medical purposes, because she had originally intended to become a doctor. But doctors had to walk a lot, constantly going up and down steps in homes and hospitals, and Florence had eventually faced the fact that she didn't want to be on her feet that much. As a result of a bout with childhood polio, Florence walked with a limp.

Florence contracted polio when the infantile paralysis epidemic tore through her hometown of Easton, Pennsylvania, at the turn of the twentieth century. Easton—established in the 1750s and located in the eastern part of Pennsylvania at the confluence of the Delaware and Lehigh Rivers—was famous for being one of the three towns chosen for the reading of the Declaration of Independence on July 8, 1776. (The other two towns were Philadelphia, also in Pennsylvania, and Trenton, New Jersey.) Born on October 6, 1897, to Barbara and George Seibert, Florence was three years old when she was afflicted. Her older brother was also a victim of the epidemic, but her younger sister, Mabel, was spared. Florence had a happy childhood, with her father providing his family a comfortable lifestyle through his business as a rug manufacturer and dealer.

FLORENCE SEIBERT

To Florence, the limp she walked with was just a part of her, and she hardly took note of it as she was growing up. The first time she gave it any thought was when her friends began to attend dances. But her limp would nevertheless have a profound impact on Florence's life. It would determine her career.

Florence excelled in school and as a result was awarded a scholarship to Goucher College in Baltimore, Maryland. While there, she decided she wanted to become a doctor. Friends and faculty advised against it because of her physical limitations, but Florence ignored them and continued to take courses preparing her for medical school. Florence realized that doctors needed to walk a lot every day and climb stairs often, but she refused to believe that something that was just a part of her should limit her in any way. When she graduated from college, she still planned to be a doctor. To earn money for graduate school, she accepted her former chemistry teacher's offer to work as her assistant in the chemistry lab of Hammersley Paper Mills in Garfield, New Jersey. Women were being accepted at the plant because of the number of men who were off fighting in World War I.

The pain and tiredness that resulted from Florence being on her feet all day convinced her that the rigors of being a doctor would indeed be too hard on her. But the work Florence did in the chemistry lab interested her, and she decided she had found her calling. She wanted to be a biochemist and she wanted to work in a lab, but not in an industrial enterprise like Hammersley Paper Mills. Florence felt she was best suited to be a research scientist. Papers she cowrote with Dr. Jessie Minor, her former chemistry teacher, on the chemistry of wood pulps and cellulose, were published and well received in the scientific community.

After working at the paper mill's laboratory for two years, Florence obtained a scholarship for postgraduate work at Yale, where she studied under Lafayette B. Mendel, one of the discoverers of vitamin A. Florence began research into why some patients experienced what were called protein fevers after they were injected with protein solutions that contained distilled water. Although her assignment was to find out which proteins caused the fevers and why, Florence instead discovered that the distilled water was actually the culprit.

After earning her doctorate in biochemistry in 1923, Florence accepted a position teaching pathology at the University of Chicago. She also worked as an assistant at the Sprague Memorial Institute, a research lab associated with the university and headed by H. Gideon Wells, a pioneer in the chemical aspects of immunity.

While at the institute, Florence discovered that although current techniques being used to distill water removed bacteria from the water, toxins the bacteria made before they died remained in the steam droplets created by the distillation process. Florence solved the problem by inventing a trap to catch the droplets. Patients no longer ran the risk of getting a fever from an intravenous injection. Florence was awarded the Ricketts Prize from the University of Chicago for her invention. Her innovative work brought her to the attention of another doctor who worked at the institute, Dr. Esmond R. Long, who asked her to join his research team.

Dr. Long was conducting research on tuberculosis through a grant from the National Tuberculosis Association (NTA). When it was founded in 1904, NTA was the first health organization to focus attention on conquering a specific disease. By 1920 the association sponsored many research programs throughout the States, with much of the needed funding for the programs coming from the sales of Christmas Seals, adhesive labels people stuck on their envelopes during the Christmas season. Although an American institution, the concept of Christmas Seals was begun in Denmark in 1904. While delivering mail, postal clerk Einar Holboll came up with the idea of the seals as a way to help the needy children he saw as he made his rounds. The postmaster and the king of Denmark approved the concept, and the first Christmas Seals bore the likeness of Denmark's queen and had the word *Julen* ("Christmas" in Danish) on them. The seals caught on right away, and more than four million were sold the first year they were available.

The first American Christmas Seals were designed in 1907 by Emily Bissell as a way to keep a sanatorium for the treatment of tuberculosis operating. Emily borrowed $40 to have fifty thousand Christmas Seals printed, and she ended up raising $3,000 for the sanitarium. The next year the NTA and the American National Red Cross made the sale of Christmas Seals a national program, and the seals were sold at public post offices for a penny. By 1920 the program was run exclusively by NTA, and proceeds from the sales of seals were used to support research programs such as the one Florence joined at the Sprague Memorial Institute.

Sprague Institute was one of many labs throughout the country where scientists worked on tuberculosis research through grants from the NTA. Each laboratory worked on a different aspect of an overall research plan. When Florence joined Dr. Long at the Sprague Institute, their objective was to identify what type of substance pure tuberculin was and then be able to produce it in large quantities. The two of them began a working relationship that would last for decades and bring much success to both of them.

In 1927 Florence was joined in Chicago by her sister, Mabel, who would help Florence around the house and eventually around the laboratory. While keeping up a strenuous research schedule, Florence learned to drive a car that was specially altered for her needs. The clutch disengaged when Florence pushed halfway down on the brake pedal, and the brakes were applied by her pushing all the way down on the brake pedal.

When Dr. Long moved to Philadelphia in 1932 to become director of the Henry Phipps Institute, he offered Florence a position teaching biochemistry. Florence accepted, and she and Mabel moved back to their home state of Pennsylvania. Dr. Long and Florence continued the research on tuberculin they had begun in Chicago, with Mabel also working at the institute as a secretary. By the time she made the move to Philadelphia, Florence had identified pure tuberculin as a protein but hadn't yet been able to isolate it from the impurities that clung to it. She would accomplish this crucial breakthrough at the Phipps Institute, making the skin test for tuberculosis more reliable and therefore more effective in the fight against tuberculosis.

To learn more about separating molecules, Florence applied for and received a Guggenheim Fellowship in 1937 to study in Sweden with Professor Svedberg, who had won a Nobel Prize for his centrifuging technique. During the year she studied the Svedberg process for separating molecules, Florence also was able to study a new process that separated molecules by passing them through an electrical field. This was called electrophoresis, and the apparatus that accomplished it was invented by Professor Tiselius, another pupil studying with Professor Svedberg.

Through a grant from the Carnegie Foundation, Florence was able to install one of these apparatuses in the lab at the Phipps Institute when she returned there in 1938. By applying what she had learned in Sweden, Florence became a specialist on separating proteins. She was one of the first scientists in the States to master the techniques of ultracentrifugation and electrophoresis to separate protein molecules. After years of research, Florence developed a standard dosage of PPD, or PPD-S, in 1941 and was awarded the Garvan Medal from the American Chemical Society in 1942. First Lady Eleanor Roosevelt presented Florence with a National Achievement Award in 1944 for her work.

Florence remained at the Phipps Institute until 1959, when she retired with emeritus status. She and her sister then moved to

St. Petersburg, Florida, where Florence continued to do research. Florence was a consultant to the United States Public Health Service, and she published her autobiography, *Pebbles on the Hill of a Scientist,* in 1968. The role bacteria might play in certain types of cancer caught her interest, and she started working on cancer research. Florence began to experience medical complications in 1989 as a result of the polio she contracted as a child, and she passed away on August 23, 1991, in St. Petersburg.

Although she was only four feet, nine inches tall and walked with a limp, Florence was a woman of great stature. During her career she authored or coauthored more than one hundred scientific papers. The technique she created to purify distilled water meant that patients no longer ran the risk of incurring a fever when they received an intravenous injection. Her work in this area would prove to be of tremendous significance when blood transfusions became standard medical procedures.

It's impossible to say how many lives have been saved worldwide by Florence's ability to isolate PPD and create a standard for the tuberculosis skin test, but it surely is a very large number. With the perfected test, people were more accurately diagnosed and more likely to receive additional testing and treatment if necessary, greatly reducing the likelihood of full-blown tuberculosis developing. Florence's work in separating protein molecules would also inspire countless other scientists to experiment with new techniques.

Because Florence was determined not to be defeated by a disability she acquired in childhood, she found a way to combine her dream of being a doctor with an occupation that required less physical activity. As a scientist Florence touched many more lives than she ever could have as a physician.

MARIAN ANDERSON

1897–1993

Singer for Equality

MARIAN ANDERSON WAS MET BY POLICEMEN as she stepped from the car, and the low murmur of the crowd made her heart beat faster as she and her companions were led through the throngs of people. As they entered the passageway to the Lincoln Memorial, the group split up, and Marian and Kosti Vehanen were soon ensconced in a small room. There they were introduced to Secretary of the Interior Harold L. Ickes. He outlined the program that was about to take place, and before long Marian received the signal telling her the time had come.

She and Kosti made their way to the platform, which already held the secretary of the treasury, a supreme court justice, and numerous members of Congress. Mr. Ickes introduced Marian, and she walked between the pillars of the monument and down its marble steps. The crowd seemed to spread as far as Marian could see, and the sheer impact of the number of people she saw was overwhelming. The emotion made her feel as if she was choking, and she momentarily feared that no words would come out when she opened her mouth.

MARIAN ANDERSON AT THE
LINCOLN MEMORIAL IN 1952

But her years of experience kicked in, and Marian's beautiful contralto voice reached out to the crowd of seventy-five thousand people who surrounded the Lincoln Memorial in Washington, D.C., on Easter Sunday in 1939. The people before her certainly had come to hear her sing, but that was not the only reason for the huge attendance at the free concert Marian gave that day. The concert was also a statement against the racial prejudice African Americans of the time were subjected to in America. Marian had originally planned to hold her recital in Washington at Constitution Hall, but the Daughters of the American Revolution (DAR) owned the hall, and they didn't allow African Americans to sing in buildings they owned. When word spread that the international singing sensation Marian Anderson had been denied the right to sing at Constitution Hall, First Lady Eleanor Roosevelt resigned from the DAR. The publicity that ensued grew larger, and Marian was invited by Secretary Ickes to give a free concert from the steps of the Lincoln Memorial on Easter Sunday. Arrangements were made to also air the performance on the radio.

Suddenly Marian was at the center of a debate focusing on the separate but equal treatment of African Americans that was currently prevalent in America. The DAR's refusal to allow her to sing at Constitution Hall wasn't the first time Marian experienced racial prejudice, and she hadn't sought out the attention the involvement of Eleanor Roosevelt brought. All Marian wanted to be known for was her singing, not her color. But once circumstances pushed her into the national spotlight, Marian performed as she always did— with grace and dignity.

Tall and exquisitely dressed, Marian looked regal in a black velvet dress with a mink coat draped around her shoulders. She led off her concert with the national anthem, followed by an aria and "Ave Maria," and then three spirituals. Her beautiful voice captivated the crowd, who showed their appreciation with thunderous applause and shouts. Marian was moved by the tremendous reaction, and although she hadn't planned to say anything, she told the crowd, "I am overwhelmed. I just can't talk. I can't tell you what you have done for me today. I thank you from the bottom of my heart again and again."

Two decades before the Civil Rights Movement would insist African Americans be treated the same as whites, Marian Anderson was a vocal lightning rod for racial equality because the beauty of her voice demanded it. African Americans and whites alike shared Eleanor Roosevelt's outrage that such a voice should be denied the chance to be heard, and many felt Marian Anderson proved that African Americans were as talented as whites.

But Marian did not seek out the racial controversy her being denied the right to sing at Constitution Hall created. When she found out the foremost concert spot in Washington was not available to African-American performers, she was more sad than angry, and she hoped her manager would be able to find another location. She only realized the implications of the situation when she saw the headlines of a San Francisco paper reporting that Eleanor Roosevelt had quit the DAR because of it.

She was amazed that anything to do with her could cause such fervor, and she wasn't at all comfortable with the public spotlight that followed. Reporters hounded her constantly, but Marian steadfastly referred all questions to her manager. When the invitation came to sing in public at the Lincoln Memorial, Marian's affirmative response didn't come quickly or easily. She wasn't a person who liked a lot of show, and she was uncomfortable with the role of a crusader of any kind. But after much consideration, Marian realized her personal feelings were not as important as her responsibility to represent her race in a favorable way, so she agreed to the concert. The fame that resulted from the controversy, combined with the beauty of Marian's voice and her gracious manner, led to Marian becoming a symbol of hope that one day racial prejudice would no longer exist in America.

A few months later Marian was awarded the Spingarn Medal by the National Association for the Advancement of Colored People (NAACP). First Lady Eleanor Roosevelt presented her with the award, which was given to the African American who had achieved the most during the year. In March 1941, Marian received the Bok Award from her hometown of Philadelphia. The Bok was given annually to a citizen that the city was most proud of, and Marian was the first African American to receive the prestigious award. She used the $10,000 prize to set up a scholarship fund to help musicians of all races attend music school. The scholarship was close to her heart, because when she was younger Marian had been denied the chance to attend music school because of her race.

Marian was born in Philadelphia on February 27, 1897, to John and Anna Anderson. The Andersons moved in with John's parents when Marian was about two years old; soon after, Anna gave birth to another girl, who they named Alyce. The family rented a nearby house after a third daughter, Ethel, was born. The Andersons formed a happy though financially poor family. Marian's father worked at a downtown farmers' market and also sold ice and coal in their neighborhood. Anna Anderson had been a teacher in Virginia, but she couldn't find similar work in Philadelphia, so she ended up taking in laundry to bring in extra income.

Marian's parents sang around the house, and Marian often joined in. She heard her first choir when her father took her to Sunday services at the nearby United Baptist Church. Marian joined the junior choir when she was six years old, and her innate talent soon led to her singing in front of the congregation at the Sunday service. Her love of music blossomed, and she convinced her father to buy a piano. The family had no money for lessons, so Marian taught herself and was soon able to play simple tunes. She was inspired to become a better piano player when she peeked in the window of a house she passed one day where wonderful music was being played and saw an African-American woman at the piano.

The serene life of the Andersons came to an abrupt end when Marian's father incurred a head injury at work and soon died. Marian and her family moved back in with her father's parents, where Marian's aunt and two cousins also lived. Marian's mother cleaned houses during the day and took in laundry to support her three daughters and pay their share of the rent.

Marian always planned to pursue music as a career. Throughout her teens she sang for the United Baptist Church choir, which was often invited to perform at other venues. Marian was a contralto, but she could sing in any range, and she filled in whenever a choir soloist was absent. Marian's talent caught the attention of the famous African-American tenor Roland Hayes when he heard her sing at a gala concert at the Union Baptist Church. He was so impressed, he arranged for Marian to study with his former voice teacher in Boston. Unfortunately Marian's grandmother had the last say in all family matters; she felt Marian sang just fine without lessons, so Marian remained in Philadelphia.

While in high school, Marian began receiving invitations to perform solo, and she became confident enough in her singing to charge $5 per appearance. In time Marian became convinced she needed voice lessons to fully develop her talent. Mary Saunders Patterson, an African-American soprano, agreed to coach her for free, and for the first time Marian began to think about the technical aspects of her singing. She learned how to project her voice, and Mrs. Patterson encouraged her to consider attending music school.

Marian decided to gather some information on one of the music schools in Philadelphia, so one day she stood in a long line waiting her turn to talk to the young girl behind the registrar's window. But when Marian's turn came, the girl looked right past her and addressed the person behind her. Taken aback, Marian stood to the side as the young girl waited on everyone else in line. When Marian was the only one still standing before the window, the girl rudely asked what she wanted. After Marian told her she had come for a registration form, the girl replied "We don't take colored" and slammed the window shut.

Marian was shocked into silence by her first experience of racial prejudice. She left quickly, and the only person she discussed the incident with was her mother, who shared Marian's reserved way of dealing with setbacks. The two decided that if Marian was meant to be a singer, God would see that it happened. Not wanting to risk more humiliation, Marian dropped the idea of going to music school. To further her training, she began taking lessons with Agnes Reifsnyder, a contralto whom Marian worked with for the next two years. But Marian's third vocal teacher, Giuseppe Boghetti, had the greatest impact on her career. Boghetti was a widely known voice teacher, and he accepted Marian as a student immediately upon hearing her sing in 1920. To raise the money Marian needed for her lessons, a gala concert that included Roland Hayes performing a solo was held at Union Baptist Church.

Under the tutelage of Giuseppe Boghetti, Marian mastered the art of breathing and developed the full range of her voice. She also was introduced to many of the songs that she would sing throughout her career. Although her singing quality was tremendous, Marian lacked training in foreign languages, a fault that showed when she sang the French, Italian, and German songs concert singers were expected to master. Marian worked hard to correctly pronounce the foreign words, but she began to wonder if she would need to travel to Europe and immerse herself in the languages to truly conquer the nuances of the words she was singing.

Boghetti would remain Marian's voice coach for years, and her mentor until his death in 1941. Once Marian graduated from high school in June 1921, she was able to begin touring. Billy King, an African-American pianist Marian had worked with from time to time since they had met in 1915, was her accompanist. Many of their engagements were at black colleges and churches in the South, and they were sometimes refused lodging and segregated when dining and traveling. Marian tried not to be affected when prejudice made touring more difficult. The performance was always her first prerogative, and she needed to be without tension to sing her best.

As her experience and reputation grew, Marian was able to charge $100 for singing engagements. When a house across from Marian's grandmother's house came up for sale, Marian's career was going so well that she and her mother decided to buy it. Her rich voice was brought to the general public when Marian made her first record in December 1923 for Victor Talking Records of Camden, New Jersey, singing "Deep River" and "I Am So Glad."

Marian's career hit a major bump on April 23, 1924, in New York City when she gave a concert at the Town Hall in Manhattan. Rather than igniting her career the way Marian hoped, the audience was sparse, and she wasn't happy with her performance. Neither were some of the critics, who especially criticized her lack of proficiency in singing foreign languages. Marian was devastated—she agreed with the critics' assessments. She returned home to Philadelphia and contemplated ending her musical career. She even stopped her lessons with Boghetti. But eventually her love of singing, and the need for the income it provided, brought Marian back to work. She increased her efforts to learn French, Italian, and German and began touring again.

Hard work and dedication paid off when Marian beat out more than three hundred other singers to win the honor of performing with the New York Philharmonic Orchestra in Lewisohn Stadium on August 26, 1925. This time she received positive reviews, and Marian gained national recognition. Soon after the concert, Arthur Judson, one of America's premier concert managers, convinced Marian to sign with his company, promising her better bookings at higher fees. At Judson's suggestion, Marian began to study with Frank LaForge, a well-known voice coach who concentrated on teaching Marian German lieder, or art songs. Lieder was still her weakness, and her studying served to convince her that she needed to travel abroad to study and master the nuances of European languages. Marian began saving her money when the higher fees Judson had promised materialized but the better bookings did not.

Feeling her career was stagnating, Marian sailed to England in the late 1920s, where she studied German lieder with some of the best teachers in that country. Marian returned to the States to tour, but she was disappointed when she once again found herself singing in the same venues she had performed at in the past. She longed to travel to Germany to study lieder, and her chance came when she was awarded a fellowship by the Julius Rosenwald Fund, which had been established to help African Americans further their education. Arrangements were made for Marian to rent a room from an elderly German couple, the von Edburgs, and to receive voice lessons with Michael Raucheisen, a respected German teacher. Marian bought a language book and worked with Herr von Edburg reading and translating German every day. The immersion in German society worked; Marian finally became comfortable with the words of the German lieder she had been singing for years.

Marian's European fame began with a concert she gave in October 1930 in Berlin. The recital was such a success that Marian caught the attention of Helmert Enwall, the director of Scandinavia's largest concert management company. Enwall arranged recitals for Marian in the capitals of Oslo, Stockholm, Helsinki, and Copenhagen, and her renown overseas grew. Although at first Marian returned to the States for the concerts arranged by the Judson management, she eventually decided to tour in Europe exclusively. Marian felt her career was stagnant in the States, confined to the same places where she had always performed, while she was being booked at prime concert halls throughout Scandinavia, elsewhere in Europe, and the Soviet Union.

After a concert she gave in Paris in June 1934, Sol Hurok introduced himself to Marian. Hurok, an internationally known American concert manager, told Marian he wanted her home country to be able to appreciate her beautiful voice. Marian wanted that also, and Hurok became her manager after she arranged to be released from her contract with the Judson company. It was agreed that Marian would return to America in December 1935, by which time Hurok would have concerts booked for her.

During the summer of 1935, Marian attended the annual Salzburg Music Festival, where her growing stardom piqued the interest of noted musicians from across the world who gathered for the festival. When the Italian conductor Arturo Toscanini remarked after hearing Marian sing, "What I heard today one is privileged to hear only once in a hundred years," her talents were lauded worldwide.

Marian's first concert back in the United States was scheduled for December 30, 1935, at New York's Town Hall. This was the same place where Marian had performed her disastrous recital in 1924, but this time she was confident of her voice and her foreign pronunciations. Now that the concert date was set, Marian had to decide whether Kosti Vehanen, the Finnish pianist who had accompanied her throughout her European tours, or Billy King, her pianist on her previous tours in the States, should accompany her. If she picked Kosti, Marian knew some whites might react negatively to a white man working for an African American. She also knew some African Americans might not like that she picked a white man to play for her rather than a man of her own race. Marian was friends with both men, but she decided to make her choice on the basis of music alone. She chose Kosti and hoped racial considerations would not overshadow the music she planned to present.

The first reminder Marian had of the racial inequality that existed in America was when Sol Hurok could not book her a hotel near Town Hall. She stayed instead at the YWCA in Harlem, just as she had when she played the venue ten years earlier. But this time Marian took a taxi to the hall rather than riding the trolley. And this time her performance was a critical success. She wowed her audience again at Carnegie Hall in January 1936, and Marian's career in the United States was reborn. Marian was pleased with Sol Hurok's management of her career, especially the care he gave to picking the right venues and marketing her tastefully. The two of them began a long friendship built on mutual respect for each other's talents and strength of character.

After her engagements in America, Marian toured successfully across Europe and South America. When she returned to the States, Sol Hurok had her booked at more than one hundred concerts in more than seventy cities. Her eminence grew as she played in prestigious halls to critical acclaim, and she often made history as the first black performer to perform on a stage in the South. When Marian played in front of segregated halls, she always bowed to her own people first when she made her entrance onto the stage.

But even while she was making African-American history, she was still subjected to racism from time to time, in the North as well as in the South. Although she was presented the keys to Atlantic City, she was not able to book a hotel to stay in the city overnight, and sometimes people refused her service or treated her rudely. Marian ignored the racism, held her head high, and kept singing and winning people over by the sheer beauty of her voice and the dignity she displayed. She made history again when she gave a private recital at the White House for a small dinner party hosted by President Franklin D. Roosevelt and his wife.

MARIAN ANDERSON

But it was Marian's Easter Concert at the Lincoln Memorial in 1939 that wrote her into the pages of history books. The concert was broadcast over the radio, and for years people would come up to Marian and tell her how hearing her sing that day had affected them. After the concert she was invited to perform publicly at the White House during a visit by the king and queen of England, making history yet again.

Marian married her boyhood sweetheart, Orpheus "King" Fisher, in July 1943, and the two settled on a farm in Connecticut. In 1955 Marian again made history by being the first African American to sing a solo with the Metropolitan Opera Company. Her autobiography, *My Lord, What a Morning,* was published in 1956, and in 1957 she was named by the Department of State as a goodwill ambassador to Asia. In June 1958 President Dwight D. Eisenhower appointed Marian as a delegate to the United Nations. She sang at President John F. Kennedy's inauguration in 1961; two years later, the president presented her with the Presidential Medal of Freedom.

Marian continued to give concerts and recitals, and as her prominence and influence increased, she progressively made concert halls treat all audience members more equally in regard to seating and ticket availability. Eventually Marian refused to perform in any racially segregated hall. She retired to her farm in Connecticut after her farewell tour, which ended on Easter Sunday in 1965 at Carnegie Hall. Her contributions continued to be honored when she received a congressional gold medal from First Lady Rosalynn Carter in 1978 and the Eleanor Roosevelt Human Rights Award in 1984. No doubt one of her favorite awards was the Grammy Lifetime Achievement Award she was presented with in 1991, since she always wanted to be known primarily for her singing. Marian passed away on April 8, 1993, but her beautiful voice lives on in her recordings.

RACHEL CARSON

1907-1964

Illuminating Ecologist

RACHEL WAS OVERCOME WITH EMOTION as she recalled the praise William Shawn of the *New Yorker* magazine had heaped on her manuscript when he had telephoned that afternoon. The tears on her cheeks were not in response to words of praise from a man whose judgment she admired or because what she had worked on for four years was finally to be published. They were caused by Rachel's realizing she had succeeded in conveying her message about the dangers of pesticides in terms the average reader could understand.

Rachel, a biologist and best-selling nature writer, felt an obligation to alert the general public to how the indiscriminate use of pesticides was hurting nature, and how harming nature would consequently harm humans. William Shawn's accolades convinced her that she had been able to put her message into terms a person without a science background would understand. She would finally be able to listen to a bird sing and know she had done all in her power to make sure birdsong, and all the beautiful sounds of nature, continued for future generations to enjoy.

But the moment of emotional release didn't last long, and Rachel quickly returned to her normal state of quiet composure. Her mind raced with all the details to be taken care of before the manuscript would be complete. William Shawn wanted her to work a bit more on the third chapter—the one where she explained all the pesticides covered in the book—to make it even easier for a lay person to read, and she had two more chapters to complete. She also needed to compile all the documentation she had gathered during her research. Rachel knew this documentation would be the key to the book's success—what she was saying was happening as a result of pesticide use was controversial, and she had no doubt that the chemical industry would use every method at its disposal to discredit her message.

Silent Spring, as Rachel titled her work, had consequences beyond alerting the general public to the dangers of pesticide use. It ushered in the environmental movement, first in the United States and then around the world. Her words awakened the world to the simple truth that man's actions have consequences on nature, and that what affects nature will ultimately affect man.

The success of Silent Spring lay in how Rachel was able to explain such a complicated scientific subject in words her readers could understand and how she was able to prove her case by citing irrefutable evidence. Her supporting documentation was included as fifty-five pages at the back of the book, and before publication she sent chapters of her book to respected scientists and asked for their feedback. Rachel painstakingly ensured that the message of Silent Spring was beyond reproach. She had to—she wasn't sure she would have another chance to convince the world of the truth she saw so clearly. Rachel was ill—she suffered from a multitude of health problems, with cancer heading the list. Her poor health had beset the completion of Silent Spring with delays, but in the end, the timing of the publication helped catapult it to success.

The *New Yorker* ran the first of three condensed installments of *Silent Spring* on June 16, 1962, and reader response beat all previous records. Interest in Rachel's subject intensified in mid-July, when the public was outraged by the news that pharmaceutical companies had attempted to market the drug thalidomide in the United States despite the fact it had caused birth defects during its use overseas. Only the persistence of one scientist at the Food and Drug Administration, Dr. Frances Oldham Kelsey, had kept thalidomide from approval for use in the States. The general distrust of drug companies that resulted from this news was further fueled by the voracious public campaign the chemical industry waged to discredit *Silent Spring*.

By the time the book was published by Houghton Mifflin on September 27, 1962, it already enjoyed intense media attention. Its importance in the mind of the nation was obvious when President Kennedy was asked at a press conference in August if the government was planning on reviewing the long-term effects of the widespread use of pesticides, and he made reference to Rachel Carson's book in his affirmative answer. *Silent Spring* spent the fall of 1962 on the *New York Times* best-seller list, and it reached an enormous number of readers as the Book-of-the-Month Club's October selection. By December 1962 the book had sold more than one hundred thousand copies, and more than forty bills regulating the use of pesticides were introduced in state legislatures across the country.

Although the chemical industry tried to fight back, Rachel's message in *Silent Spring* was assailed as the truth when President Kennedy's Science Advisory Committee released its report *Use of Pesticides* on May 15, 1963. Rachel's calm appearances on television documentaries and while giving testimony before government panels and Senate subcommittees during that year put to rest the attempts the chemical industry had made to paint her as a hysterical woman. Rachel also responded to her critics in an article printed in the September/October issue of *Audubon Magazine*. In it, Rachel

RACHEL CARSON ADDRESSES THE SENATE IN 1963

reiterated the argument that echoed throughout her book: She was not against the use of all pesticides; she felt some could be used, but they should be available only after adequate research was done to determine the effects the pesticides would have on nature.

The success of *Silent Spring* was bittersweet. Beset by medical problems, Rachel died of a heart attack on April 14, 1964, at the young age of fifty-six. It was during her last public speech, in October 1963, that she first used the word "ecologist" to define herself and gave the definition of ecology as a science that studies the interrelationship of organisms and their environments.

Her efforts to alert the public to the dangers of pesticides would result in people throughout the world becoming more aware of the environment around them and the effect their actions could have on that environment. The movement she began accelerated quickly, and on April 22, 1970, twenty million Americans observed the first Earth Day. In 1972 DDT, one of the pesticides Rachel considered the most lethal to nature and man, was removed from the market. Within ten years of its removal, the decline in populations of certain birds, which had been attributed to the spraying of DDT, had stopped, and species that had been facing extinction were no longer in danger. No doubt Rachel would have considered her greatest triumph to be that the silent world bereft of birdsong and nature she warned of in *Silent Spring* had not come to pass.

A love of nature developed early in Rachel as she grew up on sixty-four acres of land outside Springdale, Pennsylvania. Springdale was less than twenty miles from Pittsburgh, located in the western part of the state, and her parents had settled there in 1900. Born May 27, 1907, Rachel was the third child of Robert and Maria Carson. There was a substantial difference in age between Rachel and her siblings. Her sister, Marian, was born in 1897, and her brother, Robert, was two years younger than Marian. When Rachel was born, her father was forty-three years old and her mother was thirty-eight.

With Robert traveling often trying to make a living selling insurance and with Marian and young Robert attending school, Maria spent most of her time with Rachel. The two began a close relationship that would last their lifetimes. Maria had been a teacher before she married Robert in 1894, but laws of the time didn't allow married women to hold teaching positions, and Maria had given hers up. Instead she acted as a teacher to Rachel and used the expansive land the family lived on to show her child the wonders of nature. Once Rachel turned one year of age, she spent time outside every day, exploring the grounds with her mother and learning about nature. The family's two-story clapboard house shared the hill it sat on with an orchard, and Rachel often heard the horns of steamboats and paddleboats navigating on the nearby Allegheny River.

Maria was an active participant of the nature-study movement that had become popular around the turn of the twentieth century. The movement was a response to the industrialization that was occurring in cities throughout the United States, and its purpose was to minimize the effects of urban growth by making sure children learned to appreciate and love nature. Rachel's hometown was a good example of the growth that was occurring across the nation. When Maria and Robert moved to Springdale in 1900, the town had about 1,200 people living in and around it, but by 1910 the population had doubled. Although the major industry in the area was coal mining, companies involved in iron, steel, oil, and timber were beginning to dot the banks of the Allegheny River, and the air in Springdale was punctuated by the offensive odor that emanated from the town's glue factory.

The nature-study movement found an avid pupil in Rachel, who also discovered she shared her mother's love of books and writing. Growing up, she always felt she would be a writer, and *St. Nicholas* magazine confirmed her belief in her abilities when the popular literary children's periodical published the stories she began to submit when she was just weeks away from her eleventh birthday. Rachel felt her career had truly begun when the magazine paid her a penny per word for a story she wrote on St. Nicholas, and she would write for the magazine until she was in her mid-teens.

Rachel excelled in school and, unlike her siblings who both dropped out of school after tenth grade, traveled two miles each way on an unreliable trolley every day in order to complete her last two years at Parnassus High School in New Kensington. She graduated at the top of her class in 1925 and won an annual $100 tuition scholarship at Pennsylvania College for Women, a private college located sixteen miles from Springdale in Pittsburgh.

Even with the scholarship, sending Rachel to college was a financial strain on her family. Although the family owned quite a bit of land, they were often strapped financially. Her father's job as a salesman paid commission, not a salary, so income was sporadic. He would eventually take a part-time job with the West Penn Power Company, a huge utility located at the eastern edge of town. To supplement the family finances, Maria taught piano and sold piano music, but it was not uncommon for the family not to be able to pay a bill when it came due. The additional money needed for Rachel's room and board was raised by Maria, who sold apples from the family's orchard, tutored extra students, and even sold the family china to make sure Rachel got to college.

Since Rachel knew she wanted to be a writer, she selected English as her major. But her academic plans took a huge turn when she took her required science course in her sophomore year and discovered the field of biology was a perfect fit for a girl who loved nature as she did. Rachel greatly admired Professor Mary Scott Skinker, who taught the class. Over time, the two forged a friendship that would last their lifetimes, and Mary would more than once play a pivotal role in Rachel's life. Not realizing that a love of writing and a love of biology could be combined, Rachel switched her major to biology when she had only three semesters to complete until graduation. Despite having to fulfill many extracurricula requirements, Rachel graduated magna cum laude from Pennsylvania College for Women on June 10, 1929. After graduation she worked as an intern for six weeks at the Marine Biological Laboratory at Woods Hole on Cape Cod, Massachusetts, a position she had been nominated for by Mary Skinker.

Woods Hole, a small village located on a peninsula on the southeastern tip of Cape Cod, was a gathering spot for naturalists who came to study the aquatic life that teemed off its shores. Its pristine shores stood in sharp contrast to the polluted air that had descended over Pittsburgh and Springdale as industry grew. Some days the sun could hardly be seen over Pittsburgh because of all the soot and ash in the air, and Rachel's hometown of Springdale always smelled of sulfur, a byproduct of the area's coal industry. The Allegheny River was being polluted by industrial waste as Pittsburgh became known as the iron and steel capital of the world.

When Rachel saw the ocean for the first time as she traveled to Woods Hole, the spark that had been lit within her when she had found a fossilized shell on the family's land was reignited. Her internship at Woods Hole allowed her to explore the sea that she had always found fascinating, even as she grew up in landlocked Pennsylvania. After the internship, Rachel began graduate school at Johns Hopkins University in the fall of 1929. Just weeks later the country was shaken by the Great Depression. To ease financial strains, in the spring of 1930 Rachel's parents rented out their house in Springdale and moved into a house Rachel rented thirteen miles from Baltimore. Eventually Rachel's divorced sister, Marian, and Marian's two daughters, Virginia and Marjorie, also moved in. Marian was a diabetic, and Rachel's father was frail, so it was up to Rachel to find a way to support herself, three other adults, and two children while she continued graduate school.

She taught summer school at Johns Hopkins and also obtained a part-time position teaching biology at the University of Maryland. After completing her thesis, Rachel earned her master's degree in marine zoology on June 14, 1932, but financial constraints forced her to drop out of school in the winter of 1934 without obtaining her doctorate degree. Her position at the University of Maryland ended in 1933, and Rachel's only income for almost two years came from her teaching during the summer at Johns Hopkins. During this time she tried to supplement her income by editing some of her earlier poems and short stories and sending them to major magazines. Although she received only rejection slips for her efforts, her love of writing was rekindled.

Mary Scott Skinker would once again change the course of Rachel's life when she advised her to take the civil service exams in zoology. Mary had left the academic world and was working for the government, and she felt Rachel should be ready to apply for a position with the government if one opened up. Rachel took the tests and scored quite high on all of them, but no immediate job openings were available. Rachel's father died around this time, and finances were so tight that Rachel and the rest of her family sent his body home to Canonsburg, Pennsylvania, for his sisters to bury, but they did not have the resources to attend the services.

Rachel's financial situation began to turn when she landed a temporary part-time job at the Bureau of Fisheries, which would later become known as the Fish and Wildlife Service. The job allowed her to combine her loves of writing and nature by writing scripts for a public education series called *Romance under the Waters,* fifty-two short radio programs on marine life. She drew on the research she did on the scripts to begin writing articles for the *Baltimore Sun* newspaper that first appeared in March 1936. When the temporary job writing scripts was over, her boss, Elmer Higgins, decided to keep her employed part-time writing for the department. Higgins would become her mentor, and he felt an essay she wrote and titled "The World of Waters" was so good he encouraged her to submit it to the prestigious *Atlantic Monthly* magazine. Rachel followed his advice to try to have the piece published, but she chose to send it to *Reader's Digest* rather than *Atlantic Monthly.*

On August 17, 1936, Rachel was hired full-time at the Bureau of Fisheries as a junior aquatic biologist. Rachel's high scores on the civil service exams won her the job. She was overqualified but extremely happy to receive the annual income of $2,000 the job paid. She conducted research and wrote brochures and reports on fish conservation that were aimed at the general public.

Rachel's contentment at work was marred by the death of her sister, Marian, in January 1937. Her mother, who was in her late sixties, and her nieces, ages twelve and eleven, were now solely her responsibility, and Rachel moved everyone to a home in Silver Spring, Maryland, where she would be closer to her job in Washington, D.C. When June arrived and Rachel hadn't heard from *Reader's Digest* concerning her story, she decided to revise the article a bit and follow Elmer Higgins' suggestion to submit it to *Atlantic Monthly*. The magazine had her change the title to "Undersea," paid her $100, and published the article in their September 1937 issue. An editor at Simon & Schuster read the article, which dealt with the relationships between creatures of the sea and their underwater environment, and wanted Rachel to write an entire book on the subject.

For the next three years, Rachel worked at her full-time job at the bureau and wrote her book in longhand at night and on the weekends. Her mother typed up what she had written during the day, and Rachel sent off her finished manuscript to Simon & Schuster in November 1940. Her book, *Under the Sea-Wind,* came out in November 1941, and it showed how everything in the sea is connected by telling the stories of three different sea creatures. Although the book received good reviews, the attack on Pearl Harbor on December 7, 1941, and the nation's focus on the war meant poor sales for the book. Disappointed, Rachel spent the next years concentrating on having magazine articles published and moving up through the ranks of the bureau, which had been renamed the Fish and Wildlife Service in 1940.

By 1946 Rachel began considering writing another book on the sea. She hired Marie Rodell as her literary agent, and Marie sold the rights to *The Sea Around Us* to Oxford University Press. Rachel submitted her final manuscript at the end of June 1950, and the book was scheduled to be published in July 1951. Unfortunately, Rachel's joy at the prospect of having her second book published was overshadowed by a cancer scare. She had a tumor removed from her breast on September 21, 1950, but was told the tumor was benign and that no further treatment was needed. She would not learn until ten years later that the diagnosis was incorrect, and by then it would be too late to eradicate the cancer.

Rachel was thrilled when William Shawn, editor of the *New Yorker* magazine, decided to buy nine of the fourteen chapters of her book and published them in a condensed three-part article called "Profile of the Sea" a month before her book published. The publicity generated by the article helped to make *The Sea Around Us* a best seller, and it spent eighty-six weeks on the *New York Times* best-seller list, leading in first place for thirty-two of those weeks. During the Christmas season, the book was selling about 4,000 copies per day, and before the end of 1952 it had sold 250,000 copies and was translated into thirty-two languages. The success of the book caused Oxford to rerelease Rachel's first title, *Under the Sea-Wind,* which also became a best seller.

The success Rachel achieved allowed her to quit her job at the Fish and Wildlife Service in 1952 and write full time. But she would face many family distractions that would require her attention. Her niece Marjorie, after having an affair with a married man, gave birth on February 18, 1952 to a son she named Roger. Rachel went to great lengths to legitimize the child by telling friends that her niece had been married for a short time. Rachel's writing would be delayed while she helped Marjorie with Roger's care and continued to care for her mother, and she would not publish her third book on the sea, *The Edge of the Sea,* until the later part of 1955. *The Edge of the Sea* would also become a best seller, but Rachel's success would once again be tinged with sadness when Marjorie died in early 1957 due to complications she developed from a bout with pneumonia. Rachel adopted Roger when he was five years old; she was fifty and her mother was eighty-eight years old.

As Rachel expended her energy caring for her adopted son and her mother, she became interested in the stories she was hearing about the effects pesticide spraying was having on wildlife, especially that some birds were dying from eating insects that had been sprayed by pesticides. As she conducted research, Rachel realized that despite pressing family obligations she needed to let the world know the irrefutable dangers of indiscriminate use of pesticides. She began writing in 1958, and the short book she originally envisioned turned into a seventeen-chapter work that systematically exposed the dangers of unwarranted pesticide usage. It would take Rachel four years to complete the groundbreaking *Silent Spring,* and its message would change the world forever.

BIBLIOGRAPHY

Sybilla Masters

Blashfield, Jean F. *Women Inventors 4: Sybilla Masters, Mary Beatrice Davidson Kenner and Mildred Davidson Austin Smith, Stephanie Kwolek, Frances Gabe.* Minneapolis: Capstone Press, 1996.

James, Edward T., ed. *Notable American Women, 1607–1950* (3 vols.). Cambridge: Harvard University Press, 1971.

Waldrup, Carole Chandler. *More Colonial Women: 25 Pioneers of Early America.* Jefferson, NC: McFarland & Company, Inc., Publishers, 2004.

Lydia Darragh

Bohrer, Melissa Lukeman. *Glory, Passion, and Principle: The Story of Eight Remarkable Women at the Core of the American Revolution.* New York: Atria Books, 2003.

Darrach, Henry. *Lydia Darragh, One of the Heroines of the Revolution.* Philadelphia: City History Society of Philadelphia, publication no. 13, 1916.

Hoehling, A. A. *Women Who Spied.* New York: Dodd, Mead & Company, 1967.

James, Edward T., ed. *Notable American Women, 1607–1950* (3 vols.). Cambridge: Harvard University Press, 1971.

Silcox-Jarrett, Diane. *Heroines of the American Revolution: America's Founding Mothers.* Chapel Hill, NC: Green Angel Press, 1998.

Margaret Corbin

James, Edward T., ed. *Notable American Women, 1607–1950* (3 vols.). Cambridge: Harvard University Press, 1971.

Silcox-Jarrett, Diane. *Heroines of the American Revolution: America's Founding Mothers.* Chapel Hill, NC: Green Angel Press, 1998.

Transcript of Memorial Service held on Margaret Corbin's 225th birthday at Letterkenny Army Depot, Chambersburg, PA, 1976.

Lucretia Mott

Battle, Kemp. *Hearts of Fire: Great Women of American Lore and Legend.* New York: Harmony Books, 1997.

Bryant, Jennifer. *Lucretia Mott: A Guiding Light.* Grand Rapids, MI: William B. Eerdmans Publishing Company, 1996.

Hill, Jeff. *Women's Suffrage.* Detroit: Omnigraphics, 2006.

Hunt, Helen LaKelly, PhD. *Faith and Feminism: A Holy Alliance.* New York: Atria Books, 2004.

James, Edward T., ed. *Notable American Women, 1607–1950* (3 vols.). Cambridge: Harvard University Press, 1971.

Kops, Deborah. *The Women Suffrage Movement.* Farmington Hills, MI: Blackbirch Press, 2004.

Mott, Lucretia. *Discourse on Woman.* Gifts of Speech: Women's Speeches from Around the World: http://gos.sbc.edu.

Palmer, Beverly Wilson, ed. *Selected Letters of Lucretia Coffin Mott.* Urbana: University of Illinois Press, 2002.

"Report of the Woman's Rights Convention, Held at Seneca Falls, NY, July 19th and 20th, 1848": www.nps.gov.

Rebecca Webb Lukens

James, Edward T., ed. *Notable American Women, 1607–1950* (3 vols.). Cambridge: Harvard University Press, 1971.

National Iron & Steel Heritage Museum: www.graystonesociety.org.

Scheffler, Judith. *Pennsylvania History 66* (summer 1999) 276–310.

Wolcott, Robert W. *A Woman in Steel.* Newcomer address given at Union League Club of New York on December 12, 1940. Printed and bound by the Princeton University Press.

Mary Ambler

Ambler, Frank Rhoades Sr. *The Ambler Family of Pennsylvania.* Jenkintown, PA: Old York Road Publishing Company, 1968.

American Association of University Women. *In Celebration of Women.* Lansdale, PA: Women's History Week Project, 1981.

Hough, Mary P. H. *Early History of Ambler, 1682–1888.* Ambler, PA: Ambler Bicentennial Commission, 1976.

Ann Preston

James, Edward T., ed. *Notable American Women, 1607–1950* (3 vols.). Cambridge: Harvard University Press, 1971.

United States National Library of Medicine National Institutes of Health Web site: www.nlm.nih.gov.

Wells, Susan. *Out of the Dead House: Nineteenth-Century Women Physicians and the Writing of Medicine.* Madison: University of Wisconsin Press, 2001.

Elizabeth Thorn

Creighton, Margaret S. *The Colors of Courage: Gettysburg's Forgotten History—Immigrants, Women, and African Americans in the Civil War's Defining Battle.* New York: Basic Books, 2005.

Kennell, Brian A. *Beyond the Gatehouse: Gettysburg's Evergreen Cemetery.* Gettysburg, PA: Evergreen Cemetery Association, 2000; printed and bound by The Sheridan Press, Hanover, PA.

Amanda Berry Smith

Israel, Adrienne M. *Amanda Berry Smith: From Washerwoman to Evangelist.* Lanham, MD: Scarecrow Press, Inc., 1998.

James, Edward T., ed. *Notable American Women, 1607–1950* (3 vols.). Cambridge: Harvard University Press, 1971.

Smith, Amanda. *An Autobiography: The Story of the Lord's Dealings with Mrs. Amanda Smith, the Colored Evangelist.* New York: Oxford University Press, 1998.

Ida Tarbell

Fleming, Alice. *Ida Tarbell: First of the Muckrakers.* New York: Thomas Y. Crowell Company, 1971.

James, Edward T., ed. *Notable American Women, 1607–1950* (3 vols.). Cambridge: Harvard University Press, 1971.

Jensen, Carl, PhD. *Stories That Changed America: Muckrakers of the 20th Century.* New York: Seven Stories Press, 2000.

Paradis, Adrian A. *Ida M. Tarbell: Pioneer Woman Journalist and Biographer.* Chicago: Regensteiner Publishing Enterprises, Inc., 1985.

Pomper, Gerald M. *Ordinary Heroes and American Democracy.* New Haven: Yale University Press, 2004.

Tarbell, Ida M. *All in the Day's Work: An Autobiography.* Urbana: University of Illinois Press, 2003.

Tomkins, Mary E. *Ida M. Tarbell.* New York: Twayne Publishers, Inc., 1974.

Nellie Bly

Bly, Nellie. *Ten Days in a Mad-House.* New York: Ian L. Munro, Publisher, n.d.

Emerson, Kathy Lynn. *Making Headlines: A Biography of Nellie Bly.* Minneapolis: Dillon Press, Inc., 1989.

James, Edward T., ed. *Notable American Women, 1607–1950* (3 vols.). Cambridge: Harvard University Press, 1971.

Kroeger, Brooke. *Nellie Bly: Daredevil, Reporter, Feminist.* New York: Times Books, 1994.

Noble, Iris. *Nellie Bly: First Woman Reporter.* New York: Julian Messner, Inc., 1956.

Mary Engle Pennington

Nichols, Martha. *Portraits for Classroom Bulletin Boards: Woman Scientists.* Palo Alto, CA: Dale Seymour Publications, 1992.

Thomas Gale database: http://galenet.galegroup.com.

University of Pennsylvania archives: www.archives.upenn.edu.

Yost, Edna. *American Women of Science.* Philadelphia: J. B. Lippincott Company, 1955.

Florence Seibert

Chemical Heritage Foundation: www.chemheritage.org.

Seibert, Florence. *Pebbles on the Hill of a Scientist.* St. Petersburg, FL: self-published, 1968.

Thomas Gale database: http://galenet.galegroup.com.

Yost, Edna. *American Women of Science.* Philadelphia: J. B. Lippincott Company, 1955.

Marian Anderson

Anderson, Marian. *My Lord, What a Morning.* New York: Viking Press, 1963.

Battle, Kemp. *Hearts of Fire: Great Women of American Lore and Legend.* New York: Harmony Books, 1997.

Patterson, Charles. *Marian Anderson.* New York: Franklin Watts, 1988.

Thomas Gale database: http://galenet.galegroup.com.

University of Pennsylvania Library: www.library.upenn.edu.

Rachel Carson

Holmes, Madelyn. *American Women Conservationists.* Jefferson, NC: McFarland & Company, Inc., 2004.

Lear, Linda. *Rachel Carson: Witness for Nature.* New York: Henry Holt and Company, Inc., 1997.

Quaratiello, Arlene R. *Rachel Carson: A Biography.* Westport, CT: Greenwood Press, 2004.

Web Sites

ExplorePAhistory.com

Famous Pennsylvanians and Prominent Pennsylvanians: homepage.mac.com/cohora/pa.html

Friends General Conference of the Religious Society of Friends (Quaker): www.fgcquaker.org

Historical Society of Pennsylvania: www.hsp.org

National Women's Hall of Fame: www.greatwomen.org

National Women's History Museum: www.nwhm.org

Pennsylvania Historical Society: www.pa-history.org

Pennsylvania Historical and Museum Collection:
www.phmc.state.pa.us

Pennsylvania People: www.cbsd.org/pennsylvaniapeople

ABOUT THE AUTHOR

Kate Hertzog resides in Mechanicsburg, Pennsylvania, where she works as a freelance editor and proofreader. She shares her life with her husband of twenty-seven years, Tim, and their Maine coon cats, Dexter and Dillon.

Angela Tyrrell

Kate began her career as an inventory analyst who helped coordinate the systematic updating of the supplies for the Trident submarines, and she was bitten by the publishing bug when she went to work as an inventory analyst for Book-of-the-Month Club. From there Kate moved on to become a book club manager for the McGraw-Hill professional book clubs. When she left McGraw-Hill in 1996, she decided to establish her own business and perform freelance editorial work from home. Kate is the author of *Insiders' Guide to Gettysburg,* a travel and relocation guide to the famous battlefield town.